Salt Water Fishing Is Easy

Salt Water Fishing Is Easy

By

JERRY SYLVESTER

*Angling Authority and World Record
Holder for Striped Bass*

Illustrations by

JAMES M. WILCOX

THE STACKPOLE COMPANY
Harrisburg, Pennsylvania

Library of Congress Catalog Card Number: 56-7898

*Printed and bound in the United States of America
by* THE TELEGRAPH PRESS, *established 1831*
Harrisburg, Pennsylvania

Introducing Jerry Sylvester

Jerry Sylvester was born in Port Deposit, Maryland in 1896. When he was three months old his parents returned to Italy where he was raised on a farm. Twice during his early years he narrowly escaped drowning but he was not infected with a fear as often happens to children who have a harrowing experience. On the contrary, he grew up to have a love of the water.

The family returned to America when he was sixteen and settled in Waterbury, Connecticut. Grown to young manhood, he married and moved to New York City where he was employed by Mr. Thomas Ewing, Jr.

The Ewings had a summer place at Narragansett, Rhode Island and here Jerry summered yearly with ample time to seriously take up the art of fishing.

Leaving the employment of the Ewings, he opened a bait and tackle shop in Narragansett which, due to his proficiency in fishing, soon became the Mecca for anglers of all walks of life. They sought him out for advice on lures and tackle, for his services as a guide to the best fishing spots and for instruction in fishing. He was constantly recommended by sports editors, veteran fishermen, former pupils and, on request, the local police as the man to see in regards to anything pertaining to angling.

During World War II he was a checker at the Quonset Naval Air Station and it was on July 24, 1944 that he caught a world record striped bass for light tackle and eighteen pound test line, a fifty-seven pounder.

Through thirty years of fishing, by actual tabulation, Jerry Sylvester has caught 22,005 striped bass.

Dedication

This book is dedicated to my wife, Edna, a cheerful fishing widow for thirty years, who has encouraged me in my fishing and who has been of great aid to me in my tackle shop in Narragansett.

This book is also dedicated to the thousands of salt water fishermen who spend many days and nights trying to land the BIG ONE.

Acknowledgment

I wish to express my appreciation to James M. Wilcox for his thorough and conscientious work on the manuscript and format of this book.

I wish to extend my sincere thanks to Marie P. Fish of the Narragansett Marine Laboratory for her services in editing the genera and species of the fish dealt with in this book.

And my sincere thanks to the sports editors and writers whose testimonials are being used, and to Mr. Edward L. Coman for his excellent letter.

Preface

Fishing is easy. This book has been written in hopes that it will be of aid to the beginner and a helpful review for the experienced salt water angler. While my personal fishing experience has been limited to the east coast of the United States, I know from friends, all experienced fishermen who have fished the Gulf of Mexico and the West Coast, that the same techniques used along the Atlantic seaboard are equally successful in the other waters. Therefore, while this book deals with fish of the Atlantic, the fishing principles are applicable to the Gulf and the Pacific.

Many millions of dollars are invested each year in the sport of fishing, more money than is spent on all other sports combined, spectator sports included. The angler naturally hopes to realize on his investment by catching fish, but regardless of the outcome of his efforts, he is doing himself a favor the moment he wets a line. For the relaxation and peace of mind induced by fishing are most beneficial and the anticipation of a weekend of angling, in itself is a pleasure tonic no money can buy.

I want to pay tribute to the numerous newspaper fishing editors who keep in constant touch with the leading fishermen throughout the country to obtain from them information that is published in regard to weather and water conditions, where to fish, the tides, and what bait to use. This newspaper service enables the angler to indulge in this sport without undue expense, expense always entailed through experimenting with locations for fishing, bait and tackle.

It is to be hoped that the fisherman appreciates this service and that he also bears in mind that the editor can only report the conditions obtaining at the time of going to press. He is not responsible for any sudden change.

I hope more and more people will take up fishing. Having known the thrill of catching a big one, I can appreciate the excitement that is in store for the other fellow. And since fishing painlessly teaches relaxation, patience and good sportsmanship, I believe that the sport improves the disposition and makes for better neighbors and citizens.

Fishing affords a pleasant escape from the treadmill of the office, factory and shop; it relieves the tension of present day living while satisfying the competitive urge in all of us. It helps to solve problems and improve one's general well-being and outlook on life.

My wife, Edna, contends that a large fish caught will accomplish what many a wife is unable to do, i.e. lift a worried or just plain cantankerous husband out of himself into a fair resemblance of a pleasant human being. So, to exasperated wives I say, "When he goes off the beam, shoosh him out of the house to go fishing."

And finally, due to the varied prices of tackle and equipment, the sport is well within the means of all of us. Fishing is far cheaper than doctor's bills, so get out in the God-given fresh air and . . . FISH.

Jerry Sylvester

A Letter

To Whom It May Concern:

If degrees, similar to those granted by colleges and universities were awarded to fishermen for knowledge and efficiency in coastal fishing, Jerry Sylvester would have an imposing and creditable array of them.

America uses superlatives such as *expert, authority, master,* and often unjustifiably so. To say Jerry Sylvester is a *good* fisherman, no other adjective is needed to emphasize his ability. That Jerry is a *good* fisherman no one, not even his most envious competitor, would deny. To my knowledge, particularly in quest of the Striped Bass, he has no superior.

During my thirty-five years' residency near the Rhode Island coast I have known most of the ablest devotees of the "salty" phase of piscatorial art. They caught fish at times, plenty of them, but nowhere near the number that have been caught since their day. For Bass, they would fish only in "white water." To-day, due to innovations in tackle and broadened knowledge of the habits of fish, not only are more fish caught but record catches are more frequent, thus emphasizing the excellent fishing waters along the Rhode Island coast.

In my opinion, based on knowledge and experience, I know that Jerry Sylvester, by his own successes and his contribution of ideas for improvements in tackle, has done more to popularize coastal fishing in Rhode Island than any other person. His favorable reputation extends from Maine to Florida.

For many years Jerry has been *the* source of information, and many of the recognized fishermen of today—strong-hearted fellows—owe to no small degree their efficiency to association with him or to knowledge gained from him. Therefore, it is fortunate for all of us that Jerry decided to write a book and tell us, authoritatively, how, when and where to catch fish in Atlantic waters.

EDWARD L. COMAN

Wakefield, R. I.

xi

Contents

CHAPTER 1

※

Fishing Rigs and Tackle

MANY EXPERTS whom I've met are very particular about the rigs they use, maintaining that fish will shy off from an unusual rig. They insist that leaders be not less than eighteen inches and of a special gut or wire, that the diameter of the small swivels must meet certain absolute specifications, that certain colors are taboo, and so on.

I am sorry to disagree, but with thirty years of fishing experience I've come to use any rig that, at the time, seems suitable to meet the conditions under which I am fishing. I take little stock in the contention that fish become skittish upon seeing a rig that does not conform exactly to specifications and will refuse to take the lure.

During the spring of the year when catching Stripers is a very uncertain business, I've frequently altered my rig. I attached to my line a second, smaller, short leader hook—designed purely for Flounder—about six inches above the sinker. I figured that since the Stripers were not taking my lure, a Flounder possibly would take the second hook. And often I've caught a Striper on this short leader hook, generally as I reeled in to examine my bait. Obviously the change in rig—the addition of the small hook—did not frighten the fish. Had it done so he would not have struck at all.

On several occasions I've lost my rig, a big fish breaking my line, and, wanting to continue fishing, I looped two hooks onto the line, spaced far enough apart so they would not tangle in the water. With this arrangement, bearing no resemblance to a Striper rig, I caught Stripers.

It is always best to fish with the proper equipment but should the necessity arise, a makeshift rig will often bring results.

FISHING RIGS

CODFISH RIG

Use two hooks on this rig because at times Codfish will take a top bait in preference to the lower bait. Use Sproat hooks, number 6, 7, 8 or 9 with a leader of nylon or gut 10 to 24 inches in length. The lower hook is placed on the line about 10 inches above the sinker, the upper hook attached some 26 inches above the first hook. Three way swivels (not absolutely essential) may be used; they keep the bait separated and moving in the water. Use a 35 or 45 pound test line and 4 to 12 ounce sinker, depending on water action. Best bait: skimmer clams, squid and quahaugs.

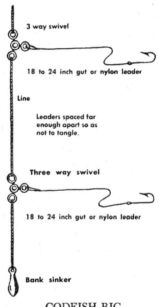

CODFISH RIG

EELSKIN RIG

To handle the Eel, it must first be killed. Place it in an empty pail then saturate it with washing soda or, second best, salt. The Eel will die in about twenty minutes. Place the dead Eel on a board or flat surface and with a sharp knife make an incision just behind the head, then cut the skin completely

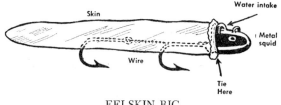

EELSKIN RIG

free from around the neck. Do *not* sever the head; it affords a grip for holding while skinning. After the incision, with pliers or fingers, peel the skin down and off, clear of the body. Insert the hook, or hooks, one inch from the tail end of the freed skin. Then work the skin up the hook shank and fasten it by means of silk or linen thread to the hole in the head of the hook. Correctly affixed, the water's action inflates the skin and it appears alive to the fish. Eels of from 10 to 14 inches in length are used for this rig.

EELTAIL RIG

Eel tails of about 10 inches are used for this rig which is easier to cast than the whole Eel rig since it affords less resistance to the wind.

Place the dead eel on a board or flat surface and make an incision as for the Eelskin rig. Then peel down the skin to within about 6 inches of the tail. Cut out all the meat exposed

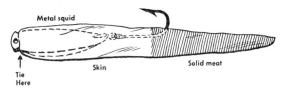

EELTAIL RIG

and replace it with a blocktin squid or a metal lure of 2 to 4 ounces thus providing sufficient weight for casting. Push the hook through the loose skin and force the barb through the remaining meat at a point 3 to 4 inches from the tail end. The whole hook must protrude. File a nick on the end of the blocktin squid, the end opposite the one containing the hook, and pull the loose skin over so that it will cover the squid. Now fasten the loose end of the skin to the squid by means of a strong linen thread, anchoring the loose skin by means of the thread and the nick in the squid.

Since the eelskin suffers little damage from rocks and sand friction, it may be kept from season to season by placing it in a jar of brine (*not* sea water) when not in use.

FLATFISH (WINTER FLOUNDER) RIG

The hooks must be small: Chestertown, number 8, 9, or 10, nylon, gut or snelled. Leaders should be from 10 to 18 inches in length; line, 10 to 20 pound test. Place the bait on the hook as illustrated. The best baits are worms and bits of clams.

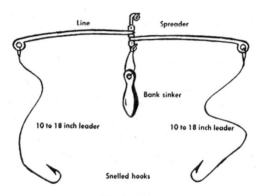

FLATFISH RIG

FLUKE (SUMMER FLOUNDER) RIG

Use a number 2, 3 or 4 snelled Carlisle hook with a 10 to 20 inch leader of gut or nylon, a 20 to 30 pound test line to which a spinner can be added 6 inches about the hook. Flounder are especially attracted by anything white moving in the water. Use a round or bank sinker of from 1 to 4 ounces but do *not* use a pyramid sinker because this sinker holds the bait still and a moving bait is best for Fluke. The exception is that the pyramid sinker is excellent for holding the bait *in place* (but not stationary) in a rip tide. This is because, due to its shape, it digs into the sand or mud bottom.

The best baits are: squid, mummies and mackerel bits.

KINGFISH RIG

The rig for this fish consists of an 18 to 36 pound test line; Sproat hooks, number 1/0; 2/0 and 3/0 with a nylon or gut leader and a sinker of from 2 to 4 ounces (often a pyramid sinker). The best baits are: shrimp, bloodworms and sandworms.

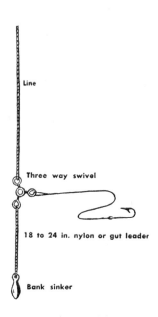

FLUKE RIG

MACKEREL RIG

Use different kinds of streamers, spoons, small plugs or bucktails. Use an 18 to 24 inch leader of nylon or stainless steel cable. Longer leaders will tangle when casting. For added weight, and as a teaser, attach an invention of mine, the Sylvester wood. This float is about 5 inches long by 1½ inches wide with a screweye at either end. Fasten the line to one screweye, the leader to the other. Then put a snap swivel on the end of the leader to permit an easy change of lure. The wood makes a commotion in the water, attracting the fish to the lure trailing behind it. The best baits are: mummies, shiners, spinners, and bits of mackerel.

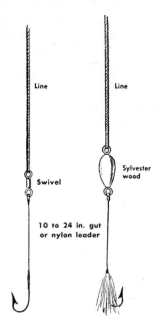

MACKEREL RIG

PORGY (SCUP) RIG

Use small hooks: 1/0, 2/0 and 3/0 with any kind of leader and a 10 to 20 pound test line. Sinker, 1 to 5 ounces. Porgy are great stealers of bait; take plenty along. Best baits: worms and squid.

Using 4/0 or 5/0 Sproat hooks, Black Sea Bass can be caught with this rig. *See Codfish rig.*

STRIPED BASS RIG

The hooks vary in size in accordance to the bait being used. For strips of squid or whole squid or live eel use 5/0 or 6/0 bass hooks. For bloodworms or sardines use 2/0 to 5/0 snelled bass hooks. For soft shell crabs or menhaden use 6/0 or 7/0 bass hooks. Leaders should be 10 to 24 inches made of nylon or gut, with a three way swivel. Sinkers from 1 to 6 ounces and the line should be 20 to 45 pound test for river, bay, boat and surf fishing. The best baits: squid, plugs, sea clams, menhaden, blood- and sandworms and soft shell crabs. *See Fluke rig.*

TAUTOG (BLACKFISH) RIG

The illustration shows the correct way to bait the hook. Use number 3, 4 or 5 Virginia tarred line snelled hooks with any standard leader 6 to 18 inches in length. Sinkers from 1 to 6 ounces. If fishing among weeds, place one hook six inches above the sinker, the second hook 15 to 20 inches above the first. Line: 36 pound test. Best bait: green crabs, fiddler crabs, razor clams, hermit crabs, blood- and sandworms. *See Codfish rig.*

WEAKFISH RIG

For either surf or boat fishing use nylon or gut leaders 3 feet in length, 2/0, 3/0 or 4/0 Sproat hooks, 2 to 6 ounce sinkers. Line 20 to 45 pound test. Best baits: bloodworms, sandworms, shrimp, squid, soft shell crabs, small plugs, jigs and feathers. *See Fluke rig.*

WHOLE EEL RIG

Use a whole eel 10 to 12 inches long. Kill it as described under *Eelskin* Rig. Then take a piece of 45 to 65 pound test linen line (or thin wire) and make a 2 to 3 inch loop in each end of the line. Fasten a hook to one end of this line by passing the line through the eye of the hook and then running the line through its own loop. Next thread the line on a "needle." This needle is homemade from a 25 inch brass rod somewhat smaller than a pencil. One end is flattened by a hammer, the other end pointed by filing or by an emery wheel. File a nick on the flattened end, on the diagonal, quite close to the base and deep enough to hold the line. The line threaded, insert the sharp end of the needle not more than an inch from the end of the eel's tail. Push the needle (and line), following the backbone, up through the body until the whole needle comes out of the mouth. Disengage the needle and tie a knot in the end of the line. Now take a piece of pliable brass or copper wire about 14 inches long. Cross this wire behind the eel's head; then push the ends, one at a time, through each gill so that they come out of the eel's mouth. Make a knot on a leader and twist both loose ends of the wire around this knot and up onto the leader, taking about six turns. The knot in the leader should be about an inch from the eel's mouth. The leader secured by the wire, fasten a hook on the other end of the line i.e. the other loop, and pull through to the desired position. This arrangement keeps the strain of casting on the head of the eel and the wrapped wire protruding from the mouth and also keeps the body hook in place.

FISHING TACKLE

The tackle herewith recommended is the gear that is best suited to the beginner and the average angler. It does not cover the complete field of fishing equipment.

CODFISH TACKLE

Heavy tackle is needed for Cod. Use a 5 or 6 foot (overall) boat rod with a 12 to 16 ounce tip, 35 to 46 pound test line, 200 yard reel, 4 to 12 ounce sinkers. The strength of the tide determines the weight of the sinker.

Generally two hooks are used. Attach one hook—Sproat number 6/0 to 9/0 with 16 inch leader—8 to 10 inches above the sinker. Attach the second hook high enough above the first so that they will not tangle in the water—about 20 inches. Codfish are generally caught by the top hook but occasionally they seem to prefer the bottom bait.

A light rod *can* be used when boat fishing, but the fish must be permitted to run with the line, otherwise he will break it. If in a party boat, this poses the problem, how to prevent your line tangling with the line of other members of the party. Hard work and skill are necessary to prevent this happening. So, to remain popular, use heavy tackle; it permits you to keep a taut line and to exercise more control over the fish.

Pollack are also caught on essentially the same equipment.

FLATFISH (WINTER FLOUNDER) TACKLE

If light tackle is used, the Flounder will provide a lively battle. Try a spinning rod and reel with a 10 to 12 pound test line or a fly rod. Also, a bait casting rod is good, together with a 100 yard reel level-winding) and a 15 pound test line. This reel automatically winds the line evenly on the reel spool thus diminishing the chances of a blacklash. Use Chestertown long shank hooks, numbers 8 to 10. These hooks are made of soft metal which, when sufficient force is applied to the leader, can be straightened out inside the fish when the hook has been swallowed deep down. Thus the hook is easily extracted. This hook is especially made for Flounder.

In general a 5 to 6 foot boat rod is recommended with a spreader which prevents the hooks tangling in the water and keeps them on the bottom. Use a 10 to 20 pound test line and sinker of from 1 to 4 ounces.

This tackle is also suited for Mackerel, Porgy, Black Sea Bass, Snappers, Weakfish and Fluke.

Fluke (Summer Flounder) Tackle

Use a 5 to 6 foot boat rod with 5 to 9 ounce tip, 100 to 200 yard reel of 18 to 30 pound test line, 10 to 20 inch gut leader and Car le hooks, number 2/0 to 4/0.

If surf fishing, use a surf rod with a 30 inch butt and 7 foot tip of 10 to 16 ounces, 10 to 24 inch gut or nylon leader and Carlisle hooks number 2/0 to 4/0.

Striped Bass Tackle

Fly rods, medium boat rods and heavy surf rods are used. *Surf rods:* 26 inch butt; 7 foot, 10 to 12 ounce tip; 150 to 200 yard reel; 25 to 45 pound test line; 24 inch gut, nylon or wire leader; O'Shaughnessey hooks, number 5/0 to 7/0. No sinker. A heavier rod has a 30 inch butt and 7 foot, 14 to 16 ounce tip. Plugs are considered the best lure for Stripers. As a guide, a 2 to 3½ ounce plug requires a 10 to 12 ounce tip. Three to five guides, depending on the length of the tip, should be spaced evenly from the tip top guide down to the butt. Guides distribute the strain throughout the rod.

For bottom fishing use the same equipment except the rod should be the heavier one; the sinkers used are 2 to 6 ounces. Boat fishing, from 2 to 12 ounces, depending on the water action.

For surf fishing, add to the rod and other tackle a New England style butt rest, a pair of light-weight waders, a four cell battery, worn either on the head or around the neck. Employ a jig bag, pocket size, to do away with the cumbersome tackle box.

Channel Bass are also caught with this equipment.

TAUTOG (BLACKFISH) TACKLE

While light tackle can be used, heavy tackle is recommended. In general, for either shore or boat fishing, use a 6 foot boat rod with a 5 to 10 ounce tip, a 150 yard reel, 30 to 36 pound test line, number 2 to 5 tarred line snelled hook, and sinker from 1 to 6 ounces. When boat fishing, Bluefish are frequently caught with this tackle.

TUNA (BLUEFIN, HORSE MACKEREL) TACKLE

Tackle for the Giant Tuna must definitely be heavy. Use a 6 foot 10 inch boat rod (overall), 39 to 79 thread line (117 to 216 test), 800 to 1600 yard reel, 10/0 to 14/0 Sobey hooks, and a 15 foot stainless steel cable or wire leader. The rod tip should be 36 ounces.

TUNA (SCHOOL) TACKLE

These little brothers of the Great Tuna run under a hundred pounds. Use a regular boat rod with a 24 inch butt and 5 foot tip of 16 ounces, a 25 to 36 pound test line, Sobey or O'Shaughnessey hooks, numbers 5/0 to 8/0, and a stainless steel cable or wire leader 5 feet in length.

SHARK TACKLE

Recommended: a regular boat rod with 24 inch butt, 5 foot 30 ounce tip, a 400 to 600 yard reel, 45 pound test line, 9/0 to 12/0 hooks or larger, 15 foot leader of stainless steel cable or piano wire. Fishing for Shark from a boat, the leader should be fifteen to twenty feet under water, so use a float to control the depth of the leader.

CHAPTER II

❋

Fishing

BLACK SEA BASS (BLACK BASS) Weight: Average 1 to
Centropristes striatus   2 lbs.
Family: *Serranidae*   Record—8 lbs.

THE SPECIES of the Sea Bass are found along
the Atlantic coast. The northern variety is the larger, running
from one to two pounds on the average; the southern averages
about a pound. They are the most numerous of the game fishes
and have sweet, firm flesh which makes for excellent eating

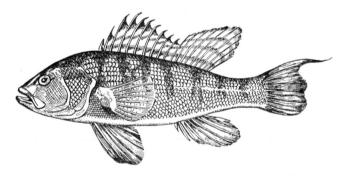

BLACK SEA BASS

and the finest of chowders. They are a hardy fish with a low
body temperature which permits them to go to deep water in
the winter to remain there, more or less immobile, until spring.
They spawn in July and August at which time, due possibly
to the pride of fatherhood, the male develops a lump on his
head and acquires bright colors.

11

During June, July and August this fish is particularly plentiful along the eastern seaboard where they are usually found in shallow water over rocky formations with weeds, ledges, sand bars and reefs close to land. They congregate in these places in great numbers.

At this time of year the only really abundant fish present in the water are Fluke and the Black Sea Bass. The Bass feeds oftener than the Fluke, so he therefore takes the brunt of the summer fishing. When the angler, at this time of year, finds other fish are not cooperative he can go after the Bass and come home with a mess of fish that would grace any table.

The Bass is a scrapper and great fun to catch. They never seem to tire, fighting up to and into the boat where they must be handled with great care, since they can inflict severe cuts on the hands with their very sharp fins. The safest way to handle this fish, when starting to remove the hook, is to either grasp it firmly by the lower lip or put fingers into the eyes and grip solidly.

Generally the larger members of the species are caught bottom fishing from boats; the smaller ones are caught from shore. Boat rods or bait casting rods are most often used with a 100 yard reel and a 12 to 25 pound test line. Use a 2/0 Virginia hook or numbers 2/0, 3/0, or 4/0 O'Shaughnessey hook on a nylon leader from 12 to 18 inches in length. The sinker should be from one-half ounce to two ounces in weight. Place one hook 6 inches above the sinker and the second hook 12 inches above the first.

This fish can be caught on both incoming and outgoing tides and while they are not choosey, taking almost anything offered by way of bait, they seem to have some preference for sea clams and squid. They gulp down the bait and, therefore, the angler does not have to be too proficient in handling his rod and line. After the first nibble he should give the fish time enough to take and swallow the bait and then set the hook, fast.

One weekend a Providence attorney engaged me to take him shore fishing for Black Sea Bass. An experienced fisherman, he had never gone out after this fish and was anxious to land some, first from shore and later from a boat. In his car we drove out to the vicinity where I knew the Bass would be plentiful, but after parking, we had about half a mile to walk before we could reach the exact spot I had in mind. We had covered about a third of the distance when I noticed that he slowed his pace, looking about him as though trying to recall something. Suddenly he stopped short.

"Hey, Jerry," he called. "I came this way once before, about a year ago, after Flounder, and I had to bury my clothes."

"Bury your clothes! Why?" I asked.

"Skunks, that's why. This place was alive with 'em and I'll bet they're still here. We'll have to take some other route."

I laughed and explained that in order for a skunk to hit one with his spray, the meeting must be head on, that he will not use his weapon unless frightened or molested and that, if he is quietly side-stepped and sidled around, he will not go into action.

He regarded me doubtfully. "We-ll, okey, if you say so, but, I'll not buy this unless you agree to buy me a new outfit if Mr. Skunk gets matey with me again."

We saw several of them but at a safe distance and reached our fishing spot without mishap. However, I believe that he set a world's record for holding one's breath while we passed through the area. P.S. He caught a nice mess of Bass.

BLUEFISH
Family: *Romatomidae*
Pomatomus saltatrix

WEIGHT: Average 5 to 14 lbs.
Record—19 lbs. 11¾ oz.

THE BLUEFISH for its size is without question the most destructive fish in the sea. It has a graceful, powerful body, pointed nose and menacing, sharp teeth. Preying on schools of mackeral, alewives, herring, cunner and butterfish, it slashes through them with a ferocity that is appalling, killing for the lust of killing long after the pangs of hunger have been satisfied. It has been estimated that a single Bluefish will destroy upwards of a thousand bait fish a day during the four months it ranges the Atlantic coastal waters.

Along the middle Atlantic coast the Bluefish is unpredictable being plentiful one year and scarce the next. And this despite the fact that weather conditions appear to be identical. No one seems to know why this is so.

Pound for pound, bar none, there is no better fighting fish than the Blue. Striking hard at the lure, he will, when hooked, stand tail end on the water shaking himself like a wet dog, trying to rid himself of the hook. Any slack line at this moment spells disaster; a taut line must be held and the rod pumped hard and constantly. Otherwise the Blue will shake the hook from his mouth and disappear into the depths.

Bluefish are caught, day or night, by either trolling or surf fishing using plugs, Japanese feathers or sea worms for lures. At times, however, when very hungry they will take practically any bait or lure and this regardless of wind and water conditions. Blues have a habit worth noting: they will return to a given

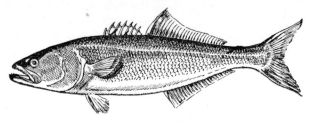

BLUEFISH

locality just before dark, or in the early morning, where they will remain feeding as long as the bait fish are present.

When fishing at night use a strung eel for best results. The eel must be hooked so that the barb of the hook and most of the shank protrude near the end of the eel's tail, for Bluefish take bait from the rear. Unfortunately, due to the violence of the strike and the sharpness of the Blue's teeth, every strike means that the eel must be replaced with a fresh one because a battered eel is worthless as bait.

Should you miss the first strike, stop reeling in for a few seconds and then proceed again. The chances are he will come back and strike again.

Small surface plugs or under-water plugs are also used successfuly for night fishing. Use a slow retrieve with a series of quick little jerks then allow the lure to drop back a few feet and repeat the process.

If trolling for Bluefish, and they are jumping around the boat but are not biting add a 2 or 3 ounce sinker to the line and the chances are you will boat a few.

If bottom fishing, use mullet, strips of squid, shadder crabs or worms for bait together with the stainless steel cable or piano wire leader not less than twelve inches in length with a three way swivel attached about six inches above the sinker. Fish with a slack line so as to give the fish every opportunity to swallow the bait. Otherwise he can shake the hook from his mouth; at this he is a specialist.

When casting into a school of Bluefish remember this: at night retrieve slowly; during the day, retrieve very fast.

The actions of sea gulls often indicate the presence of Bluefish. Many species of game fish wait for conditions to be just so before they start to feed, but the Bluefish is unpredictable. So, despite what appears to be adverse conditions, watch the gulls. If the Bluefish start, or are about to start feeding, the gulls will circle closely overhead keeping an eye on the water beneath. When this happens it is safe to assume the Blues are there and will soon begin to feed.

Do not stop fishing if the water should suddenly become rough because the Bluefish likes to feed under this condition. Should they seem to have gone, remember that they will return again a bit later to resume feeding. Before I discovered this habit of theirs, I have on several occasions reeled in and left disgusted, only later to have friends who, stayed on, show me a nice catch of Blues taken shortly after I had departed.

Be on the lookout for single Blues jumping after bait fish. Often a Blue will desert the school to forage on his own and a cast close to where he breaks will often take him.

Bluefish schools that travel along the rocky shores behave differently from the schools in the outer waters. Apparently in the early morning they feed as a school, but about day break they separate and individual fish lie in wait among the rocks for unwary bait fish.

On rocky shores, Bluefish will readily go after artificial lures, but on sandy shores the best results are obtained by bottom fishing with worms and strips of squid for bait.

It never pays to be careless with a landed Bluefish. I recall the time my friend Bill and I were fishing for Blues and he hooked an eight pounder on light tackle. Expertly he played him until the fish tired and then he brought it in. Elated over his catch and talking to me about it, he reached down to disengage the hook. It seemed to me that the fish reared up on his tail to meet the descending hand which was gripped by the thumb with a bulldog-like hold. Bill yelled and tried to free his thumb, but the fish hung on despite everything and it took several minutes for the two of us to pry him loose. Considerable damage was done to the thumb; enough to spoil the rest of the day fishing for Bill.

So when you land a Bluefish, tap him on the head, hard, with a rock or anything handy before you try to disgorge the hook. The Bluefish have beautiful, sharp teeth set in powerful jaws that are capable of giving a terrific bite.

Originally I fished for Blues using a double gang hook jig. Using this jig I continually lipped nine out of ten fish that struck and thereby lost them. So I changed to a single blocktin jig and landed ninety per cent of the fish that took this lure. The single hook apparently sank much deeper into the jaw when the Blue struck. This jig is now standard, the gang hook jig being generally abandoned.

When catching Bluefish on a hot sunny day, bury the fish in the sand in order to preserve them until you are ready to take them home. Bluefish spoil rapidly so always clean them before you depart and don't leave the "innards" on the beach for in no little time they will smell to high heaven.

Do not use a brass swivel because the fish, attracted by its glint, will strike at the swivel instead of at the lure and, since they strike with great force, you are apt to lose the whole rig and part of the line. Black swivels are best as they do not glint and attract the fish.

Almost any small feather jig is a good lure for Bluefish.

The waters off the coast of North Carolina afford one of the best localities for catching Bluefish, particularly during the month of May when they are migrating north. In the more northern waters, Montauck, Long Island, Block Island and Martha's Vineyard are the localities where the Bluefish will congregate to remain, as a rule, all summer long. Charter boat captains are aware of this and take full advantage of it. However, knowing where to find them and, once found to get a good catch, are two different matters.

Not long ago a charter boat captain came to me and admitted that while he could easily locate the Blues, he was not being too successful in having his party boat them. I asked him if, when trolling, he had advised the use of drails. He said he hadn't and seemed rather hazy regarding this technique. So I proceeded to explain to him in detail.

A drail is a half moon-shaped piece of lead 2½ to 5 inches long weighing 1/2 to 5 pounds. It has swivel eyes at either end. The line of a *second* rod or a tarred hand line secured to the boat is fastened to one eye; a short 12 inch line is fastened to the other eye. To the end of this short line is attached a snap clothes pin. This clothes pin is clipped on to the line with which the angler is fishing, from 5 to 15 feet above the lure. Now, should the angler desire to fish at a depth of 25 feet he will measure off 25 feet on the drail line and then attach the clothes pin, clipping it on the fishing line say, ten feet above the lure. When both lines go into the water the weight of the drail, which drops to a depth of twenty-five feet, will hold the lure at that depth.

When the fish strikes at the lure, the fishing line comes free from the clothes pin, thus removing the weight of the drail and relieving the fisherman of the extra weight as he pumps the rod, playing the fish, and thereby reducing the effort needed to land it.

Another excellent method for catching Bluefish, which is not used extensively, is to anchor the boat and chum with menhaden or mackerel. For bait, cut triangular strips from the fish being used for chum, each strip being from 4 to 5 inches long on the sides and 1½ to 2 inches wide at the base. Use 5/0 to 7/0 hooks, hooking the strips through the base. Fish with free line. If, however, the tide is strong, add a ½ to 1 ounce sinker to your 12 to 24 inch stainless steel or wire leader.

When Bluefish are migrating from the north, in October, the routine of work around Juno Beach and Palm Beach, Florida, takes second place to fishing as the anglers thereabouts take advantage of the first run of the Blues. Bottom fishing with strips of mullet is the usual method for catching them, but spin-casting is fast coming to the fore.

BONITO
Family: *Scombridae*

ATLANTIC BONITO (SKIPJACK, COMMON BONITO, HORSE MACKEREL) *Sarda sarda*	WEIGHT: Average 3 to 10 lbs.
OCEANIC BONITO (STRIPED BONITO) *Sarada velox*	Average 15 to 20 lbs. Record—31 lbs. 8 oz.

There are two species of this member of the Mackerel family in Atlantic waters, the Atlantic Bonito and the Oceanic Bonito. The Atlantic species, smaller of the two, has dark, oblique stripes running down from the top of the back to the stomach. The Oceanic species has bands running horizontally along the body. This fish is similar in shape to the Tuna but is more streamlined, resembling somewhat, a torpedo. And like a torpedo they glide swiftly and smoothly through the water.

The Bonito prefers offshore deep water but occasionally, carried away by the excitement of chasing bait fish, it will be found closer in to shore, generally near a breakwater.

From late June through the summer and into November the Bonito range fast and far in deep water in quest of bait

BONITO

fish. However, they are unpredictable as to season; they may arrive late, then disappear in September, or they may stay on until frigid weather. One year they will be plentiful; the following year very scarce.

Generally Bonito will be found where Tuna and Bluefish are skipping and bouncing over the water either after bait fish or just for the fun of it.

Trolling is the usual method for going after this fish. They are curious about anything moving rapidly through the water and are attracted by the wake and churn of the propeller of a reasonably fast motor boat. Fishing from or near the stern, the lines are let out from thirty to fifty feet into the wake of the boat, proceeding at a good speed. The Bonito will strike with great swiftness, taking the lure at full tilt, never slacking his pace, and once he is hooked, he must be given line and the drag applied with caution. If not given leeway something is bound to give due to the speed of both fish and boat. The Bonito fights hard and affords good sport.

The recommended tackle for party boat trolling is a 6 foot boat rod (overall) with a 200 to 400 yard reel and a 36 pound test line. Tested lures are Japanese feathers, cedar jigs and block tin squid.

One day in mid July my friend Sam Greer came to me and

informed me that Bonito were jumping inside the Point Judith breakwater, and that he'd been after them in his boat for two days but with no success. Jokingly I boasted that I could catch any fish I saw jumping and he insisted that I back up my statement then and there. I couldn't leave at the moment but the following day we went out to the breakwater; the Bonito were still there. They were bouncing over the water, glistening streaks of fish that were beautiful to see.

We got into his boat and rowed out to where they were disporting themselves. I had an 11 foot surf rod, a 200 yard reel of 36 pound test line and a Japanese feather for my lure. We both began casting and my third effort brought me a nice five pounder much to Sam's disgust. When we quit for the day I'd made good my boast to the tune of nine Bonito ranging from 3 to 9 pounds in weight. But my wrist was sore from the effort of reeling in because a slow or medium fast retrieve will not do when catching Bonito. The angler must reel in as fast as possible so that the speed of his lure will cause the Bonito to strike. This fish delights in hitting a fast moving bait at full speed.

Sam's catch was three fish, made after I explained to him what was wrong with his technique. First of all he was using plugs for his lure which do not, as a rule, attract Bonito. Secondly, he somehow could not bring himself to reel in with the speed that was necessary.

A fisherman will never forget the first time he ties into one of these muscular fighters. My first experience with the Bonito was from a party boat five of us had hired. We set out from Long Island and some twenty miles out we reached an area where several boats were chumming and fishing for Tuna. We cruised back and forth in their vicinity for the best part of an hour but had nary a Bonito strike. Then just when we were beginning to wish we'd come out for Tuna (we saw several nice ones boated) it happened. Our lines were over the stern and suddenly there was a turbulent swirl and a glistening of sleek bodies in the wake of our propeller, and, with sudden and unexpected force, all five of our lures were hit at once. To say we got a thrill is putting it mildly and we boated five Bonito ranging from 4 to 8 pounds in weight. After that strike the school departed for parts unknown; we caught no more but the savagery of the attack and the thrill of the moment more than compensated for the lack of further catches.

CHANNEL BASS (RED DRUM)   WEIGHT: Average 8 to
Sciaenops ocellatus   40 lbs.
Drum Family: *Sciaenidae*   Record—83
                                                          lbs.

While this member of the Drum family is occasionally found
farther north, the Channel Bass generally ranges from off the
coast of New Jersey to the Gulf of Mexico. Oregon Inlet, North
Carolina, is a particularly well-known locality for catching this
fish.

Similar in many ways to the Striped Bass, the Channel Bass
can be caught on top with surface lines at a depth of from

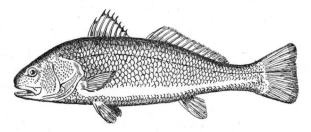

CHANNEL BASS

three to four feet, but he is essentially a bottom feeder staying
from one to two feet off the bottom. Ranging along beaches,
sluices and just beyond outer bars, they feed on soft shell crabs,
menhaden, squid and live eels. They are active from April until
the end of October and the best time for catching them is
during the four days just prior to the full moon of each month.

During spring certain wind conditions must be taken into
account along with the cycle of the moon. If a northeast, east
or southeast wind prevails, the water will be very active and
the tides fast. Channel Bass like this condition and go on a
feeding rampage, and fishing will be good if on a rocky bottom.
But if the bottom is sandy, it will be poor because wind and
tide stir up the sand and the fish cannot see the lures. Off the
North Carolina coast, in particular, a northeast wind will spoil
the sport.

Should a northeast storm blow up on the new moon, it will
continue for three days if it doesn't expire within twenty-four
hours. Having set in for a three day blow, the wind will often
shift to the southwest and will last for twenty-four hours and

then shift back again to three more days of a nor'easter. Should this cycle occur, and you can find a rocky bottom, fishing for Channel Bass will be good. Should only a sandy bottom be available, retire to the hotel, get out the cards, relax and wait until the winds blow themselves out.

Felix Fracasso, Joe and I were fishing one day on a rocky bottom for Channel Bass. The wind was from the northeast, the tide was making fast and the water was becoming too active for comfort. So we decided to quit and Joe, always one for a laugh, started back ahead of us, clowning as he went. Suddenly he took a header and went under, his feet waving in the air and every time he tried to get to his feet his head would bob under and his legs would shoot skyward. It was a comical performance to Felix and me and it was not until Joe was half drowned that we came to the realization that he was not kidding but was in real trouble. We got to him quickly and dragged him to shore.

What had happened was that the air in his waders had made his feet and legs so buoyant that they were lighter than the rest of his body and they shot into the air on each attempt he made to regain his feet. He could have righted himself by paddling hard with his hands thus keeping head and shoulders upright while pulling his feet down and under him. But he became panicky and didn't use his head in the emergency. It is good general rule not to horse around at any time when fishing.

Channel Bass and trash fish—small shark, sting rays, skates and the like—are fond of the same bait-fish. Now trash fish are far more numerous than the Channel Bass, so the fishermen using menhaden, sand crabs and squid for bait, will find that they are constantly catching more trash fish than Bass. Therefore it is advisable to use a large eel since the Channel Bass likes eel and the trash fish (excepting good size dogfish or small shark) shy away from it; they cannot swallow the eel.

Spoons are the best artificial lure but are very difficult to cast for any appreciable distance, the average cast being about fifty feet. However, by adding the Sylvester wood, far better distance can be obtained. On a still day the average cast, with the wood added, will be around a hundred feet; with the wind behind the angler, around a hundred and fifty feet.

The spoon and wood rig can be easily manipulated for either a fast or slow retrieve and it can be readily dropped back in a rip tide or in a strong undertow wave. Frequently a slow retrieve is the best for catching Channel Bass.

When surf fishing for this fish, use a rod heavy enough to support a 5 or 6 ounce sinker. This weight is often necessary because, with a tide running strong, any sinker of less weight will prove inadequate to hold the lure down. However, for surface surf fishing, the rod tip should weigh from 10 to 12 ounces. For surf bottom fishing, it should weigh from 14 to 16 ounces. Use a 200 to 300 yard reel with 36 to 45 pound test line, 5/0 to 9/0 hooks, and a 12 to 24 inch wire leader. This leader is advised because Bluefish are often around and they will cut a nylon or gut leader should they elect to go after the lure.

CODFISH (COMMON)   WEIGHT: Average 15 to 50 lbs.
Gadus callarias   Record—

TOM-COD   Average 4 to 10 oz.
Microgadus tomcod
Family: *Gadidae*

The Codfish is one of the most abundant and valuable of the food fishes in the sea. It is estimated that the annual catch is well over a hundred million pounds. To offset the terrific inroads in its population, the Cod is very prolific, the average female producing between three and four million eggs yearly from October to April and the fry are fully matured within three years.

Codfish are caught the year round with most of the fishing being done from party boats. There are, however, localities where they can be fished for from shore; Cape Cod; Montauck, Long Island, Point Judith breakwater, Rhode Island and the Pier at Belmar, New Jersey, to mention a few of the better known places.

Many fishermen assert that Cod fishing is a sport somewhat on the dull side, that the fish does not have the fight possessed by other species. In making this statement they fail to take into account that the heavy tackle used reduces the struggle between man and fish to the point where the odds are highly in favor of the fisherman. If light or medium tackle is used, it will soon be discovered that plenty of fight and know-how is necessary to boat a good-sized Godfish. Of course, fishing in very deep water, it is obvious that light tackle is out of the question because it is inadequate to haul a heavy fish up to the surface. However a *medium* rod and equipment *can* be used and good sport will be the result.

Excepting the Striped Bass, the average fisherman is accustomed to catching much smaller fish: Fluke, Blackfish, Weakfish and Porgy—to name a few. So when he eventually does decide to go after Cod, his mental attitude is not "how hard will he fight" so much as "how big will he be and what

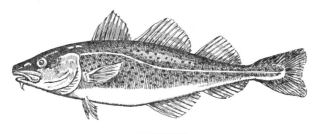

CODFISH

will he weigh?" His thrill will correspond to the size and weight of the Codfish he brings in.

Along the middle Atlantic coast there are many places where party boats may be hired, places that yearly accommodate thousands of fishermen. Galilee (Point Judith, Rhode Island) is one of these places and the second week of November found a party of ten of us sailing out from there. We had picked Galilee as our point of departure because, in this general vicinity, it is necessary to go out only a mile or two to find water not too deep and tides not too strong so that a light or medium boat rod with a 2 ounce sinker may be used. For bait we had sea clams, conchs, squid and two bushels of black mussels with which to chum.

We anchored over a ledge some two miles out and began fishing just before daybreak. We had not been able to chum these waters the night before but several boats had preceded us and their chum was keeping the Codfish close to the ledge. The moon was in the last quarter and the sea was very calm and the tide, half out, was barely moving. Not a good time to fish, for under these conditions bait fish are not active; consequently the Cod do not feed.

We started fishing, however, using the various baits we'd brought along, but our efforts resulted in catching just a few fish that were so small they hardly warranted being boated. The Cod were hitting occasionally but were not swallowing the bait. They often act in this manner while waiting for the tide to change and the bait fish to become active.

The tide changed but our luck did not. We were fishing with large pieces of bait on our hooks, mindful of the saying "the bigger the bait, the bigger the fish." But having had no success, we decided to abandon this method. Putting on smaller pieces of bait and moving our rod tips slowly up and down we began to get results, shortly landing several Codfish weighing from 12 to 25 pounds with one 35 pounder heading the catch. In every instance the fish struck as the rod tip was being *raised* after having been lowered some three feet i.e. raised from the nine o'clock to the twelve o'clock position.

Three of the boys failed to profit by our change in method because they used cut clams from which they had removed the strings instead of letting the strings remain and hang down from the hook. Noticing this, I advised them to thread the hard part of the clam onto the shank of the hook, the soft part onto the barb, and let the strings dangle. They soon caught fish.

I believe that the inside of a squid is the best bait for Cod because it attracts not only the smaller Cod but the large ones as well. In all the years I've fished for Cod I've never noticed anyone using the insides on his hook, with the execption of friends of mine I've tipped off. For some obscure reason the inside portion is always discarded. To me it is my ace in the hole; it seems to have a strong attraction for the Codfish when all other baits fail.

To prepare this bait, first slice the squid from head to tail and then hold by the head and pull the whole insides out in one piece. Thread them on the hook by piercing the hard portion two or three times with the barb of the hook and let the soft part hang below the barb. Always let the barb show; then get set for a pleasant surprise when you use this bait.

Codfish also like the meat of the conch, a large sea snail with a beautiful pink and white shell. In preparing conch for bait, pains should be taken to cut the meat extracted from the shell, into attractive looking bait. Remove the hard skin with a sharp knife and cut the white meat into strips long enough to thread over the barb of the hook and onto the shank. Thread the hard portion on first and let the soft part hang over the barb with the barb protruding. Codfish do not like the hard part; it is the soft portion they will swallow. So, if you feel that a fish has been definitely nibbling at the bait, the chances are that the soft part is damaged or gone and new bait is called for. Always have plenty of bait on a fishing trip; to skimp is poor economy; you can readily run out before the fishing day is over.

One day two of us, boat fishing for Cod, ran out of the squid we'd been using for bait. We changed to smaller hooks and caught Cunners, using small pieces of Cod we'd boated, for bait. Placed on our hooks, these live Cunners (Bergalls) proved quite effective; we continued to fish. Often, party boat fishing, I've won the boat pool using both squid, and the Cunners my companions had boated in disgust. Apparently the Cod liked the live bait as well as the squid on these occasions. Since Cunners are always around rocky bottoms and wrecks, they are a source of supply if you run out of the bait that was brought along.

If using a very soft bait such as oysters or scallop rings, tie it onto the shank of the hook with cotton thread or any handy string. The barb, of course, should protrude. I am convinced that fish take small notice of leaders, thread, lines or hooks. What *does* matter is that the proper bait be correctly placed on the proper hook.

Fish for Codfish with a slack line and do not use too large a hook. Sproat hooks, number 5/0 to 9/0 should be sufficient. Keep the bait moving constantly, for Cod will go after anything they see moving; he instinctively does not want to see something that appears edible escape him. The Codfish has been known to swallow tin cans, rings, tins and various other objects that attracted him.

A word about party boat fishing. Have confidence in the judgment of the captain. If he has anchored and chummed and you have fished for some time with no appreciable results, don't start pestering him to move to another spot. The captain has brought the boat to this spot where he believed there would be good fishing. He aims to please and earn his money and to obtain a good reputation as the man to hire when you want fish. He has his own good reasons for staying in this particular locality; he may be waiting for a change in the tide. Remember, he probably knows the waters far better than you do, so have patience. He will up anchor and move on the moment he feels that it is the best proceedure to do so, and he will explain to you why he is moving. His livelihood and reputation depend on his ability to guide a party boat to areas where fish will be caught and his customers satisfied.

Offshore wrecks, rock ledges and ridges are good locations for Cod fishing and the best time of year is during their migration in the fall and spring. While fishing is good during their migration north in May and June, it does not equal that during the months when they migrate southward—October and November. Should you decide to fish during the cold months you will find it is difficult to keep the hands warm. The best means I know of is to rub plenty of vaseline on the hands before starting out and then wear wool mittens or heavy woolen gloves. Try to keep them as dry as possible.

In regard to chum and chumming: One method is to smash, say mussels, a few at a time, and chuck them overboard, watching to see how fast they sink so as to judge from which part of the boat they should be thrown in order to establish a chum stream. The boat of course is anchored. Generally this point is from the bow and the chum stream floats past the side of the boat and out beyond the stern.

Another method is to smash up the chum in a burlap bag and add sufficient weight so that the bag, when secured and lowered over the side, will hang suspended alongside and level with your baited hook.

The porous burlap bag (or bags), containing one-half to a bushel of chum, permits the natural oils of the chum to seep out into the water and the Cod are attracted by the scent. The chum bag should be lifted and shaken every half hour, and replaced with a new one about every two hours. The natural oil is dissipated in about this length of time.

Best results are obtained if you can chum a chosen spot the night before. Cod swim about during the night looking for an area where food is plentiful; finding the chummed water they will remain in the vicinity and by morning the place will swarm with them.

AMERICAN EEL (COMMON)   WEIGHT: Average 12
Anguilla rostrata   oz. to 16 lb.
                                            Record—none
CONGER EEL
Conger oceanica

The American or Common Eel, ranging east of the Rockies
to Atlantic waters, is the only true Eel in the United States.
There are, however, various other related species found in the
Gulf Stream, off the Grand Bank, the Florida Keys and the
Gulf Coast and in the Pacific.

The Common Eel is usually darkish mud-brown on top and
a lighter brown or whitish-yellow underneath. The migration
of this fish is just the reverse of the migration of the Salmon
i.e. the Eel migrates from fresh water to sea in the autumn
and the young Eels make their way from salt water back up
fresh water streams in the spring. The spawning grounds are
located to the southwest of Bermuda.

This fish is responsible for destroying great numbers of

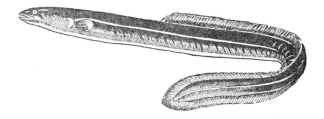

EEL

shad and herring and it is a nuisance to gill net fishermen.
Often Eels, caught in a gill net, will destroy all the other fish
entrapped with them leaving only skeletons to be brought to
the surface.

Eels are good to eat and fishing for them along the coast
from shore is a popular sport. Generally the fishing is done at
night off of breakwaters, rock jetties and over rock bottoms.
They are also caught in inlets and bays and streams but these
fish are, as a rule, smaller than those caught along the shore.

It seems to be a tradition among confirmed Eel fishermen
that the hand line be used in preference to rod and reel. And

the argument in favor of the hand line is that it is more sensitive and nibbles and bites can be felt more readily.

The natural habitat for the Eel is a rocky bottom, few being caught off of sandy bottoms; so drop your hand line close to rocks. For a bottom rig use a 45 pound test line with 4/0, 5/0 or 6/0 hooks and a three way swivel. Place the swivel about 6 to 10 inches above the sinker on the end of the line; place one hook on the swivel and then attach a second hook high enough above the first so that they will not tangle in the water. The sinker should be from 2 to 8 ounces in weight.

The most popular bait for Eels is squid. Cut the squid into a V shaped length of from 2 to 4 inches. Place it on the hook at the base of the V. Other excellent baits are soft shell crabs, shiners and mummies (chubs). Should the bait be used up, the hook can be baited with small, skinned portions of the Eel's own meat as an emergency measure.

Rod and reel can be used for Eel but the rod must be on the heavy side so as to enable the fisherman to lift the Eel from the rocks; they are too active and squirmy to gaff. Use a light Tuna rod 4 to 6 feet in length and weighing from 16 to 22 ounces. A reel of from 100 to 200 yards of 45 pound test line, together with hooks from 2/0 to 6/0 and a leader of gut or nylon 6 to 12 inches in length. Three way swivels should be used as they keep the line straight when the hooked Eel twists and rolls about.

The Eel is a scavanger eating anything alive or dead—small fish, crabs, crustaceans, shrimp, refuse and carrion—and if the bait is correctly placed on the hook it is not too difficult to catch since it eagerly seizes anything offered. Night fishing is best for Eel but he can be caught in the day time. The best time is during the last two hours of an incoming tide; they feed on all tides.

When using a kerosene or battery light at night, do not shine it directly down on the water; it will frighten the Eel away. The purpose of the light is to enable you to see to bait your hook and to find your way about.

One night Jerry Simonetti and I went to a favorite breakwater after Striped Bass. It was the last two hours of an incoming tide and we expected to catch a Striper or two. We were using surf rods of 12 ounce weight, 36 pound test line and 6/0 hooks with squid for bait. But instead of Stripers we caught Eel after Eel. Disgusted, I voiced my opinions in no uncertain terms, but Jerry was enjoying himself. Having reconciled himself to the fact that no Stripers were around, he was landing Eels as fast as he could pull them in, just for the sport of it, and then throwing them back in the water.

But since he was cutting his rig from the line on each cast—the easiest and most practical way to get an Eel off the line—we soon were running out of rigs. Two nearby anglers, fishing with handlines, stopped fishing and came over to us. They looked at our considerable catch of Eels and then one asked, "How come, you two who don't want Eels are catching 'em, and we who do, haven't caught one?"

They admitted to being beginners so I asked to see how their hooks were baited. They had been putting on chunks of squid too large for an Eel to swallow and furthermore the barb of the hook was well hidden inside the bait. I explained about cutting the squid into a V shape and letting the barb protrude. They followed my advice and soon were catching Eels.

It is a good practice to chum the area you are fishing; the chum keeps the Eels in the vicinity for a considerable time. Use crushed black mussels, clams or rock crabs.

Should the ocean become very rough on the night you are fishing, try fishing inland from a bridge or off a bank; with rough water setting in, the Eels seek inlets and bays.

A close relative of the Common Eel is the Conger Eel. This fish is purely oceanic and has been known to attain the length of eight feet and a weight of fifty pounds. It ranges the waters of the Atlantic coast as far north as Cape Cod. They can give a terrific bite, even after the head has been severed from the body, which is frequently done in order to remove the hook from the Eel's mouth. Allow five minutes to elapse before handling an Eel presumed to be dead, for the nervous system functions for about that length of time and the bite can come from reflex action.

The accepted way in which to kill an Eel, when landed, is to use a mallet with considerable force, starting with the head and pounding the length of his body to the tail.

FLATFISH (WINTER   WEIGHT: Average 1 to 3 lbs.
FLOUNDER)   Record—None
Pseudopleuronectes americanus   recorded

The Flatfish is a freak of the sea with its twisted head, alternating light and dark coloration, its clumsy method of swimming and its bulging eyes set close together on either the right side or the left side of its body. When hatched, the fish does not have these peculiarities; it does not swim in a leaning position and its appearance is that of any normal young fish. But within a few days the bones of the head twist and the

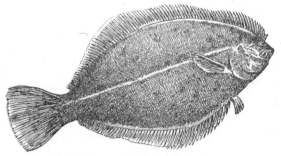

FLATFISH—WINTER FLOUNDER

under-surface eye passes to the upper side of the head to join its mate. Within a month it becomes a misshapen adult with a laterally compressed body who's upper side is a dark brown and lower side, white.

The Winter Flounder is the most abundant member of the Flatfish family which includes the Halibut, Fluke and Sole. It ranges from Florida to Maine.

The Winter Flounder is a very prolific fish, the female, during the short spawning season of from February to April, laying, on the average, a million eggs. The spawning is at night and the eggs are heavy and of an adhesive quality. The fry are hatched in about five months, generally during the month of August. They are about two inches long.

Fishermen, novice and expert alike, who have been cooped up all winter long in the city look forward to the day when the Flats begin to run. First in the spring, they usher in the fishing season. And these fish do not require too much skill to catch, so it is easy for women and children to land them. They are excellent eating in the spring if they are cleaned immediately and then placed on ice overnight for consumption the next day.

During the Winter Flounder season, which lasts from March until the end of May, there is no reason, good weather prevailing, why the fisherman should go home empty handed. If he fishes the right spots, using various baits, he should make a catch sufficient at least for home consumption.

When fishing for Flounder, use a light rod with 100 yard reel of 15 to 30 pound test line together with number 8, 9, or 10 hooks and a 10 inch leader of gut or nylon. Blood and sand worms, night crawlers, soft or hard shell clams, scallop rims, black mussells and ribbon (tape) worms are all good for bait. The ribbon worm will often attract the fish when all other baits fail. This worm is frail, brittle and reddish in color and is found by digging in the mud flats at low tide. Use them the same day they are procured as they cannot be kept alive over three or four hours.

An acquaintance of mine, a lady just taking up fishing, rushed up to me, highly agitated. She pointed to a nearby bait shop. "Do you know," she cried, "that man tried to sell me TAPE WORMS for bait. Why, last year my father nearly died from a tape worm and now he, that so and so . . ." She spluttered to silence.

I finally calmed her down by assuring her that the Tape or Ribbon Worm is in no way related to the Tape Worm that plagues humans on occasion.

A Flounder will often play with the tail of a bait (which should be dangling from the end of the hook) and if, when the nibble is felt, the rod is lifted too quickly, or with a jerk, the fish will let go. A *gentle* lift, however, encourages him to gulp the food which he sees getting away from him, and he will thus swallow the hook. So, if the fish is missed by too quick a lift, the line should be allowed to remain quiet again for about thirty seconds to afford the Flounder a second chance to take the bait. When he gives it a second try a gentle lift will probably land him.

On the third of March two of my friends joined me for our first trip of the season for Flounder. We drove to a bay where we knew the tides would not run too fast. Our tackle consisted of bait casting rods, 100 yard reels of 20 pound test line, number 10 hooks and sand and blood worms for bait.

In the spring the best spots to fish for Flounder are in the bottom holes in the middle or near the end of a bay. The best time is on the outgoing, or ebb tide, fishing until the tide starts coming in. So we anchored on a bar near the middle of the channel. I made a few casts from the end of the bar, slowly moving and stopping my bait, my rod tip travelling through an arc of about four feet. On the sixth cast I felt a Flounder suck at my bait; I raised the rod too fast and missed him. Chiding myself for being too anxious I let my bait lie still in the water and waited. Again I felt him tug at my line and this time I lifted the rod slowly and evenly and I had him. What a thrill! Just a small one but the first catch of the season. It was not long until I'd landed five Flounder; the season was on.

But my friends, having no luck whatsoever, asked me what they were doing that was incorrect. I examined their setups and found that instead of *threading* the worm on the hook they were bunching it on the shank so that it was all crumpled up with the head and tail dangling in two directions.

I explained that a worm *must* hang straight along the shank of the hook with one end dangling from the barb; it will thus appear natural to the fish. Flounder will pick at the dangling end and then when the rod tip is lifted, imparting movement to the worm, it appears that the worm is getting away and the Flounder will instinctively gulp at and swallow it even though not particularly hungry at the moment. My friends rebaited their hooks and, slowly lifting their rods when a nibble was felt, were soon catching fish.

But at this point Nature took a hand. The light wind which had been blowing into our faces, coming from the same direction the tide was flowing, suddenly strengthened and veered about so as to be blowing on our backs and *against* the tide. That did it. For the combination of wind against tide renders static the movement of the various food particles drifting in the water so, with no food floating about, the Flounder stopped feeding. With this occurrence we had to either wait for the wind to veer about again, or if it continued to blow steadily from its new direction, for the tide to change.

We waited; the tide changed and the wind held steady and we each caught several more Flounder. But suddenly the wind increased, blowing strongly and in the same direction that the tide was flowing, the water became very swift and the fish stopped feeding.

The explanation for this is simple. When water becomes too fast, the natural food of the fish—particularly the worms—drops to the bottom and remains there. Knowing that no food will be floating about in swift water, the fish—never energetic in the spring—do not bother to try to feed. Later in the season, however, when the Flounder are very active, roving about in the channels, this condition of a very swift tide will not stop them feeding. However, on a full moon tide, they will not feed freely.

On the sixteenth of March three of us started out for some more bay fishing and we reached our destination in time to start fishing about nine o'clock. We anchored over a bar in shallow water so as to fish the deep water hole which lay just beyond the bar. Our bait, carried by the tide, would move into this hole where the Flounder would be waiting for food to be washed over to them by the action of the water. About this time of March the Flounder begin to develop active appetites, so we expected good fishing.

We had picked just the right spot and we caught more fish in two hours than would have been possible had we fished for ten hours in the wrong location. Furthermore, had we anchored twenty feet in either direction, we would not have been "on" and our catch would undoubtedly been far less satisfactory. Even though considerable time may be spent in so doing, it always pays to take the time to locate the right place to fish.

The following day we fished the same place using the same bait and tackle. An identical tide was running but we caught only two Flounder. The wind was responsible for this poor fishing, for shortly after we had wet our lines, it started blowing from the northwest, the temperature dropped sharply and the fish buried themselves in the bottom. My companions decided that we were through for the day but I had a trick up my sleeve. We upped anchor and rowed slowly back and forth over the area dropping the anchor, hauling it up, dropping it again, repeating this routine for some fifteen minutes. The idea was to arouse the fish. We anchored again at approximately the same spot from which we had started the operation, and after waiting a quarter of an hour for the water to settle we began fishing again. Our tactics paid off with a nice Flounder catch to take home.

A bar, such as we fished, is formed by a sector of land that is higher than the land adjacent to it. It may, or may not, protrude above the water's surface. The *hole* is where the sides of the bar shelve down to the land beneath. The water immediately over the bar is lighter hued than the water over the hole. A bar, submerged, is located by this light-hued water; the hole is marked where the light hue merges with the darker. Fish congregate in the hole, waiting for food to be washed over the bar to them by the action of the tide. Washed over, it sinks down and is easily gobbled up.

Returning the next day to the same bay with my friends, I suggested they pick our fishing spot. They decided on the sand bar we'd previously fished, we anchored over it but three hours passed with nary a fish caught. Losing patience my friends wanted to know why, with the same spot and identical weather and water conditions, no fish were being boated.

I explained that while conditions *seemed* the same, actually they were not. Previously we'd fished the bar on the *outgoing* tide, the water flowing from *shallow* to *deep, over the hole* to which the bait fish were being carried. Today we'd been fishing the *incoming* tide, and the water was flowing from *deep to shallow* and the bait fish following the tide, did not drop down into the hole. Therefore the Flounder were not feeding here.

We had two courses to follow: either sit tight and wait until the tide changed, "thus producing the hole" again or, find another spot where the incoming tide was washing food into a hole. But this was a small channel and it had but the one bar we'd been fishing over and this was good only on the *outgoing* tide. Grumbling a bit at me for letting them fish for so long a time under the wrong conditions, my companions decided to wait; they were rewarded with a very nice catch of Flounder once the tide changed.

The first week of April found us on the shore of a bay channel that was inland about a half a mile from the ocean. During this time of spring the Flounder are moving back and forth with the tides and feeding eagerly. Judging from their activity, it would seem they were exercising, preparing for their journey out to sea, for it is at this time the Flounder moves down from back up in the bays, ocean-bent for the summer.

We walked along the shore looking for a point of land jutting out into the channel; here the tide would form a small pool of swirling water into which the natural food of the fish would be washed and the Flounder would congregate at this spot to feed. But we failed to find what we were looking for so we decided to fish the channel proper from shore.

The trick in fishing a channel is to cast into the middle thereof where the water is swift and then, moving the bait slowly, allow the action of the water to carry the line into the slacker water along the channel's edge where it is easier for the fish to find and take the hook. With each cast and retrieve the bait is covering the maximum area from swift to slack water. On the retrieve do not reel in steadily; lift the rod tip slowly and then take three or four turns on the reel; stop for about fifteen seconds and then repeat the performance. The fish generally strike as the bait is being lifted.

We had fished for nearly an hour and then my friends began complaining that the Flounder were not biting. Half-hearted nibbles and bites yes, but no real strikes and, no fish. Another half hour passed and they began to wish for different bait, made uncomplimentary remarks regarding the ancestory of the fish and blamed the hooks as being either too large or too small. And finally, since I'd caught a few, they accused me of having cornered all the luck of the party.

Discount luck as a factor in catching fish with any consistency. Occasionally a cast will land practically in the mouth of a fish and he will grab the bait but this happens so seldom a fisherman can't count on it for good fishing results for a season.

I stopped fishing in order to disabuse my friends of their evident belief in "fisherman's luck." I pointed out that their poor technique was to blame. That, on feeling a nibble or bite, they were lifting their rods with a jerk so hard and so fast that the fish had no chance to swallow the bait. They changed to a gentle lifting of the rod and soon were happy over the fish being caught.

But shortly we ran out of the bloodworms we'd been using for bait. Small and easily swallowed, worms are seldom passed up by Flounder. Our remaining baits were clams and quahaugs, and soon my companions were in trouble again. They either didn't get a strike or, when they did, they missed it completely. I noted what was wrong: they were using chunks of clam large enough to choke a Flounder had he been able to get it into his very small mouth. So I explained that clams were excellent bait for Flounder when cut into small, fish-shaped pieces about a half an inch long with some clam strings hanging and the soft portion of the clam attached to the barb of the hook; the hard portion, which the Flounder does not like, to the shank. Thus prepared, the action of the water makes the clam piece wiggle so that it appears like a small bait fish to the Flounder.

A few days later we returned to our channel, but a strong northeaster blew up; the tide ran so fast that the water quickly became so roiled that we knew the fish could see neither the natural food nor the bait we were offering them. So we accepted the situation and went home.

From the fifteenth of April until the end of May and occasionally a bit later, Flounder feed around bridges, docks and in deep holes in bay channels. If shore fishing a channel, walk until you find an area where the shallow water merges with deep water—determined by the change in color—and this is the spot to fish.

Fishing channels, bridges, docks and banks until the full moon in May, makes for a long Flounder season. In the latter part of the season the Flounder will begin to run small at these places because the majority of the larger fish have departed for open water and only an occasional big one will be caught. So, if after the larger Flounder, this is the time to switch fishing activities to the beaches. Any beach that is not too far removed from an inlet or bay is good and the best time to fish here is on the high tide. Use the same tackle and bait that was used for "inland" fishing, but the sinker must be heavier, 1 to 4 ounces, so as to hold bottom in the ocean tides.

A sand spike is almost a necessity for beach fishing, for it not only is a big aid in baiting the hook, but it also protects the rod and reel from the sand which would be picked up when the rod, otherwise, is laid on the beach. Also the hands are freed to cut bait.

About June we forget about Flounder fishing because they go out to sea not to return until fall when, during September, October and November, they are again plentiful along the beaches and in the bays.

FLUKE (SUMMER FLOUNDER, WEIGHT: Average 2 to
RUSTY DAB, YELLOW-TAIL, 8 lbs.
SAND DAB, RUSTY FLOUNDER) Record—25
Paralichthys dentatus lbs.

The Fluke, a member of the Flatfish family, is found from the South Carolina coast to Cape Cod. It is a larger fish than its relative, the Flounder, reaching a maximum length of four feet as compared to the one foot length of the Flounder. In weight it runs approximately four times heavier. In the main, the habits of the two fish are about the same. While not as abundant as the Flounder, the Fluke is frequently plentiful

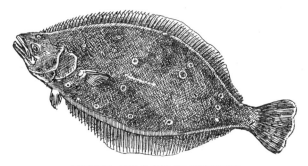

FLUKE—SUMMER FLOUNDER

along the Atlantic Coast, appearing off the shoreline from May until October. It is both a bottom and top feeder and is caught offshore: off sandy beaches with weedy bottoms, in inlets and in bays. Excellent eating, they are much sought after by fishermen who, frankly, could in most instances, improve the technique employed to catch them.

Fluke are a very curious fish and will investigate anything white or flashing in the water. They do not bite; they suck on the end of the bait dangling from the hook, drawing it into their mouths. They will take hold of the end of the bait, and if slack line is not given at this moment, they will do one of two things. Either they will quickly let go of the bait or they will, before the rod can be lifted to set the hook, rush off for deep water holding the bait but *not* the hook in the mouth. Too often the angler, feeling the tug at the end of his line, will jerk the rod, attempting to set the hook, only to find that the

Fluke and part of his bait are gone. Given proper slack the fish will hook himself.

Just before dusk Fluke come to the surface to feed upon live bait fish and will continue feeding on after dark. Since they feed this way, put a large float on your line set so that the bait will lie about three and a half feet deep in the water. Just let the float drift about on the waves. However, if you prefer to cast, use a bait casting rod with a reel of from 100 to 200 yards, 20 to 36 pound test line and a ½ ounce sinker with a streamer or bucktail lure. Cast and then retrieve as slowly as possible. A short shank hook with wire leader, or a long shank hook must be used for Fluke because they have exceptionally sharp teeth that can weaken or sever a gut leader as they fight.

For bait use shiners, minnows, eel, squid or Fluke strips. Occasionally strips of bergall or mackerel will prove to be satisfactory. The best artificial lures are small plugs, feather streamers, spinners or pearled hooks. The last two are excellent because their flash and shimmer attract the Fluke from quite some distance away. A bass flat tail plug is frequently taken by the larger Fluke.

Many fishermen out after Striped Bass are surprised at landing a large Fluke. They forget that the Striper and Fluke like many of the same lures and baits.

If fishing for Fluke from a rowboat, just let the boat drift about with the waves unless you know where there is a sandy bottom with weeds, in which case, anchor and fish there. Once anchored keep the bait constantly moving.

A word about boat fishing for Fluke or any species of fish. Unless you or your friends are experts on the water do *not* leave a bay to fish an inlet or outside in open water if the water is really rough. Inlets are treacherous, day or night, but particularly at night. So if there is any doubt at all as to the advisability of setting out, ask some one who knows rough water, and respect his advice even though it may mean curtailing your fishing. I know I have saved quite a few people from drowning, fishermen who were sensible enough to take my advice and follow it.

One day several of us were fishing a sandy bottom, edged with weeds, off a rocky shore. We were using shiners for bait and catching some good-sized Fluke. But the bergalls were very active and it was not long until our shiner bait was gone, stolen by those little thieves. Having no other bait, I sliced some strips from one of the Fluke we'd caught, planning to use them for bait. A couple of boys scoffed at the idea but I induced them to cut the strips into small, triangular shapes about 3 to 5 inches in length, and to pierce the base of the triangle with the barb of the hook. Baited this way the strips hung straight down.

The Fluke were not particularly active, so in order to attract them, we continually moved our rod tips up and down, reeling in a few turns and then letting the line out again on the next lift of the rod. We had the feel of the weight of the sinker on the line so could tell with each lift if there was any extra weight added, *i.e.* if something had quietly taken the bait. A few minutes after putting on my Fluke bait I felt that extra weight on my line; I lowered the tip some three feet and then slowly raised it again. The makeshift bait was a success; a large Fluke was firmly on, having hooked himself.

Occasionally that perfect fishing day will come along, a day when fish will be caught regardless of what bait is used. Such a day generally follows a storm, which, bringing fast tides and roiled water, causes the natural food of fish to bury itself in the bottom until conditions improve. Being deprived of their food for several days the fish become very hungry. When the weather lifts, they have voracious appetites and prefect fishing conditions exist.

After such a storm newspapers report big catches of many species of fish caught with every imaginable bait or lure. The lucky angler who caught a big one tells his friends about it, attributing his catch to his skill and the particular bait *he* used. Dame Nature is seldom given credit for an assist, which she certainly rates. She is responsible for the fish being unable to eat for the duration of the storm, and for several days after. She also clears the weather, which finds the fish with such voracious appetities that they will strike at anything that appears to be edible. So, following a "perfect-condition-day-of-fishing," don't assume that any old bait will do for the next time out; it won't. The proper bait for the particular fish you are after *must* be used for consistent results.

KINGFISH (KING WHITING)   WEIGHT: Average 1 lb.
Menticurrhus saxatilis   Record—6 lbs.
DRUM Family: *Sciaenidae*

The Kingfish belongs to the Drum family of fishes which includes, along with other species, Weakfish, Silver Perch, Channel Bass, Drums, Ribbonfish and Croakers. The Kingfish is found off the Atlantic Coast from New Jersey to Maine. During the months of May, June, July and August surf fishing for this fish is a very popular sport and it is particularly good along the New Jersey and Long Island shoreline. The best time to fish for them is

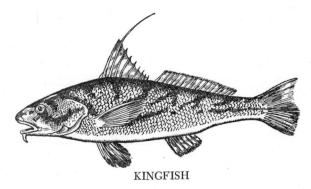

KINGFISH

during high tide when they are following the tide and moving closer into shore. They are also caught in bays and inlets.

The Kingfish is small, seldom exceeding three pounds in weight, but this lack in size is compensated for; they are delicious to eat. Essentially a warm water fish, Kings will seek deep water of fifty to sixty feet if a sudden cool day occurs and the surface water becomes chilled.

Kingfish will first nibble at a hook and then suddenly strike with the force of a ten pound Bluefish. For tackle, use a regular boat rod and a 150 to 200 yard reel with an 18 to 36 pound test line. Small hooks such as number 1 or 2 Sproat or Carlisle are needed, with nylon or gut leader and a sinker of 2 to 4 ounces in weight. The pyramid sinker should be used, as it sinks into the sand and bottom mud, thus holding the bait steady.

Since Kingfish are bottom feeders, place a single hook from 2 to 6 inches above the sinker on the end of the line. Should you wish to fish with two hooks, place the second hook 6 to 8 inches above the first hook.

Frequently one member of a party will catch more fish than the other anglers. When this happens—all things being equal—it is generally because the "lucky" fisherman is using more bait than his companions. He is not loading his hook; quite the contrary. After he has felt a number of nibbles with no subsequent bite, he is discarding the bait and replacing it with some that is fresh. Then again, if after a reasonable length of time he has felt neither a nibble nor bite, he will reel in and replace the bait, now somewhat stale, with fresh bait. Stale bait is merely bait that has been in the water long enough for it to lose its juices which are dissipated by the action of the tide. Stale bait does not possess an attraction for fish that fresh bait does; so don't be sparing with bait.

One day late in May a friend of mine invited me to go fishing near Jones Beach, Long Island. Arriving at our destination, I found that a party had been made up, several members of the Rockaway Surf Club joining us. I was not aware of the fact that my friend had done some advance advertising in respect to my fishing ability and that a secret competition was on, the Club members wagering amongst themselves as to which one would outfish me.

We proceeded to our fishing grounds and, this being a strange locality, I took considerable time studying the water. I wanted to find "Kingfish" water, *i.e.* deep water or "hole" near the shore. I found the spot I was looking for and when the day's fishing was done I'd caught more fish than the rest of the party combined. The reason for my success was this: my companions had been casting over a long bar and into *shallow* water instead of into the deep water or "hole" where the Kingfish were feeding.

It pays for a fisherman to learn early where the deep water lies, and to remember that when waves are breaking normally along a shoreline, they indicate shallow water. Detecting deep water may take a little time, but it is there where the fish are found, lying in wait for the bait fish to be washed over to them.

One night in September, some twenty years ago, I took a young boy on his first fishing expedition. We went to an inlet where I hoped he would catch a Weakfish or a Bass. Not being too experienced myself, I'd provided but one bait, strips of squid. Using surf rods, 200 yard reels of 27 pound test line with 18 inch gut leaders and pyramid sinkers, we cast into the current and let the sinker move along the bottom until it stopped in the slack water on the edge of the current. The squid was cut into 5 inch strips and we got frequent big, hard bites but no real strike, and no fish. Deciding that small Bass were biting on strips that were too big for them I cut our remaining squid into 2 inch strips. The result was surprising; we immediately began catching *Kingfish* of a very respectable size. The expedition was a success; the boy never forgot that night.

Almost yearly, the middle of September will find the boy, now a grown man, returning to that spot trying to recapture the thrill of his first fishing night, and a mess of fish as well. He has since learned that the Kings that bite at night are generally the larger of the species.

MACKEREL (COMMON)   WEIGHT: Average ½ to
Scomber scombrus   3 lbs.
                                      Record—8 lbs.

The Common Mackerel is found in the open waters of the Atlantic from Labrador to Cape Hatteras. During the months of May and June it spawns along the coast of Long Island and the New England States. A single female lays as many as a half million eggs, which, deposited in the water, are promptly

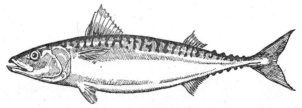

MACKEREL

fertilized by the male Mackerel. The eggs float near the surface of the water and the young Mackerel, or fry, hatch within a few days. By fall they are about seven inches long, but four years is required for them to reach maturity and a foot in length with a weight of about a pound.

This fish is especially relished and preyed upon by Cod, Whales, Mackerel Sharks, Bluefish and the Porpoise. Squid make great inroads upon the young. The Gannet, diving down, wings folded, from a hundred feet in the air, takes a heavy toll of the Mackerel.

The best months for catching this prolific fish are April, May and June and again in September, October and November. They migrate north in the summer and south in the winter.

The party boat is the most popular method, using various chums such as manhaden, shiners and strips from the Mackerel itself. While other chums can be used effectively, the menhaden chum is highly recommended. Throw the menhaden overboard in small quantities at close intervals so as to make and form a chum stream that will attract and keep the Mackerel in the vicinity.

Once the chum stream is established, and has attracted the Mackerel, it seems that almost any bait or lure will serve to catch them. They will take live bait, artificial lures and occasions are known to have seized a bare hook. Various fresh water spoons and shiners are good lures, but experience has proved small feathers or shiny chrome-plated jigs to be the best. Good sport will be had if light tackle is used such as a fly rod or bait casting rod with a level winding reel of 100 yards of 10 to 20 pound test line with 1/0, 2/0, or 3/0 O'Shaughnessey hooks with a 3 foot nylon or gut leader. With light tackle the odds are not so heavily in favor of the fisherman.

If boat fishing, let the line down to a 15 to 20 foot depth. A sinker of from ½ to 1 ounce in weight should be used, depending on the action of the water. The hook should be baited with a strip of Mackerel if not satisfied with the lures being used or if you have run out of live bait.

Mackerel, in common with several other species of fish, are particularly attracted by anything shiny that is moving through the water, so lift and lower the rod tip continuously. Should the boat be rocking to any appreciable extent, employ the lazy fisherman's method; just let the motion of the boat do the work while you hold the rod steady on the gunwhale. On feeling a bite, do not raise the rod tip too quickly, because, if given half a chance, the Mackerel will hook himself.

Surf casting for Mackerel is done along the beaches, from docks and from breakwaters, using a fly rod or small bait casting rod. Use a streamer fly or a small spoon attached behind a wood float. The wood float is attached to the line by a screw eye on one end; the lure is attached to another screw eye on the opposite end of the wood by means of a leader from 18 to 20 inches in length. If the leader is too short the lure will not go deep enough, if too long, it tends to tangle with the line.

This wood I invented was of necessity; I wanted something

that would add just the right weight so that, using a surf rod, I could cast a light lure—feather, streamer, fly or very small plug. The wood is from 2 to 5 inches in length.

One advantage of using this light tackle is that the smaller fish can be caught as well as the larger ones.

Until comparatively recent years, little surf casting for Mackerel was done. This was because the lighter rods now in use had not come into vogue; it was thought that only heavy surf rods and tackle could be used, casting from the shore.

One day I was fishing for Mackerel and I had tried everything in my tackle box with zero results. Disgusted, I pondered the situation and decided that possibly a lure with more shine than any I had with me might be the answer. Not being far afield, I returned home and, over the protests of my wife, took a silver-plated spoon from a drawer. I drilled a hole in either end, fastened a hook in one end and returned to the beach. I had caught one Mackerel, foul-hooked, from which I cut a small portion. I cut it into a triangular shape about one inch in length and inserted the hook of my makeshift lure in the base. The whole contraption looked somewhat like a minnow hooked through the lips. On my third cast I knew that my troubles were over; I landed a three-quarter pounder. And then, more Mackerel, evidently attracted by the shine of the spoon, continued to take my lure until I caught all the fish I wanted.

Each day presents a new and different problem for the fisherman so it is necessary to experiment to some extent with lures, baits and methods of retrieving so as to obtain the best results. There are no exact tables or hard-fast rules that can be followed. The spoon experiment, I'll admit, was rather on the drastic side.

Always take note of the water; it influences the feeding of the fish. Try to remember what condition you noted, how the fish were biting, and apply this observation to your next fishing expedition. In time you will acquire a practical overall knowledge which will save time, trouble and experimenting, and will produce fish.

Some days the Mackerel will take only small flies or small spoons; other days they can be caught only by reeling in fast; again, a day comes when one must reel in slowly with little jerks of the rod tip. On another occasion they may be feeding deeper than usual, so a long leader, say 24 inches in length with additional weight—a sinker of from ½ to 1 ounce—must be used.

This in order to carry the bait down to the desired depth. At times a nylon leader is best suited; other times a wire cable or piano wire leader. The nylon leader, being light in weight, tends to keep the bait on the surface; the heavier cable or piano wire will carry it down. And the action of the water always plays a part in each instance.

When fishing with bait fish, such as small herring or silversides, use any type of float you like and set it on your line so that the hook will hang in the water at a depth of from 3 to 4 feet. (Consult the illustration of the Fluke rig which is also used for Mackerel. How you place the bait is very important.)

Mackerel have very small, hard mouths so, once hooked, there is small chance of losing them and they are easily lifted into a boat without the need of a net. Due to their small mouths, and small stomachs, any chum being used should be ground into an almost powder-like consistency so that it will be easy for the Mackerel to swallow and also so the fine particles will not fill the fish's stomach causing him to bog down and stop feeding, his appetite temporarily satisfied.

If enjoying a good catch, do not take home more than you can use. A fish will live if thrown back into the water within a reasonable length of time unless he has been hooked through the eye, or his "innards" torn out when disengaging the hook.

POLLACK (BOSTON BLUES)   Weight: Average 5 to
Pollachius virens   20 lbs.
Family: COD *(Cadidae)*   Record—not
                                                      recorded

The Pollack, member of the Cod family, ranges from Cape May to Nova Scotia. In recent years it has become increasingly sought after by fishermen, both sport and commercial. This is due to the fact that several other species of popular fish have become somewhat less plentiful than formerly and the Pollack, once considered "trash" by commercial fishermen, is now coming into its own as a desirable fish to catch. They are plentiful and excellent to eat.

One drawback to the Pollack is that it spoils easily. It is a good policy to bury the fish in the sand promptly after it is caught, particularly on a hot, sunny day, in order to preserve them until time to take them home. If boat fishing, promptly put them in the water either in a mesh fish bag or on stringers. The Pollack must be cleaned in about five hours.

On the new moon in October go to your favorite fishing spot; the Pollack, a punctual fish, should have arrived. The best time for catching it is either just before dark or shortly before daybreak. At these times it is most active in chasing bait fish. Should you arrive at your fishing grounds a bit early and visibility is poor, the presence of the Pollack is easily established. Traveling in schools, it causes quite a commotion, splashing the water in pursuit of its prey.

The water conditions seem to have little effect on the Pollack's feeding habits, barring calm waters when it is in-

POLLACK

clined to feed more actively at night than during the day. However, on occasion, it will feed actively throughout the day; this is the exception.

Sea gulls will aid in locating Pollack. They will circle over an area where they are, or rest upon the water, waiting for the fish to start feeding, hoping to pick up morsels of discarded or dismembered baitfish.

Casting from shore for Pollack is difficult. In my experimental days with this fish, surf fishing was in its infancy; not many anglers indulged in it. But I persisted, spending many fruitless hours and making many trips to tackle shops, buying different lures. Finally I found one that brought fairly consistent results: a 2 to 4 ounce piece of wood about 3 inches long. It was tied to the line, with or without a leader, and the lure was attached some 20 inches below the wood by an 18 to 20 inch leader.

Prior to this discovery my efforts had netted me one medium-sized Pollack, foul-hooked through the tail, plus an improved vocabulary concerning the Pollack and its ancestors. Undoubtedly the Pollack gave me a harder time than any other species of fish I've gone after.

Today there are many different, improved lures designed to catch this fish, but I still use the lure I've mentioned, for through the years, season after season, night and day, it has proved satisfactory. I see no reason to change.

When the water is quite wavy, there are two good methods to use. First, using a wood-bucktail-trailer lure, cast out and let the wood lie still on the waves whose movement will impart a natural, fish-like motion to the lure that will be some twenty inches below the surface. When the fish strikes, set the hook gently and then reel in. The second method is to cast and then reel in very slowly until the jig reaches the shallow water at your feet. Then let the underwash of the waves carry the float back out again a few feet where the fish, having followed the lure, will take it. Generally this type of fishing is done after dark and the small and average-sized Pollack will respond to these techniques.

And now for the big ones. Change from the wood-bucktail-trailer lure to a small plug of about 1½ ounces in weight. The smaller Pollack are not interested in this lure to any appreciable extent but the big ones are. Making this change in lures, you will catch fewer fish but those which are caught will be on the large size; the ones which ignore the wood-bucktail, will take to the shiny plug.

When a large one is hooked, always remember to take plenty of time in landing him because if you hurry the process a twenty to thirty pound fighting fish can easily break the rod or line and the rig will be lost.

Tackle for Pollack should be either a regular surf rod or a bait casting rod; a 100 yard reel with 20 pound test line and the wood-bucktail lure or small plug. No sinker is used.

One night, about twelve o'clock, I was awakened by the ringing of my telephone; two of my friends wanted to go fishing for Pollack. Sleepily I agreed and when they arrived at my place an hour or so later I was ready. We set out for a spot I knew we could reach in time to start fishing just before dawn, an excellent time when they commence feeding in earnest to continue on until daylight sets in. With broad daylight they will, as a rule, go out to deep water to return again at dusk to feed with the tide.

There had been two days of dry, cool weather with an off-shore northwest wind, and this condition always causes calm water. Now, during a northwest wind and calm water, the bait fish will gather along the shoreline, bunching up more than is usual. With the coming of broad daylight, the water being calm and clear, the bait fish are able to see for a considerable distance and can detect the on-coming Pollack, intent on making a meal of them. Alerted in time, the bait fish will scatter and be on their way, outswimming the larger fish, and the Pollack will not pursue them. The only occasion on which the Pollack will persist in the chase is when the water is cold. A lowered temperature affects the smaller fish, slowing them down to the extent that their bigger adversaries can catch them without undue effort.

Bearing in mind the weather and water conditions, we knew that the bait fish would not be around for long. We wasted no time in getting our lines into the water. We were using bait casting rods with 100 yard reels, level-winding, and 20 pound test lines with the wood-bucktail lure and an 18 inch nylon leader. The bait fish were beginning to scatter, so we cast into them and reeled in very slowly, stopping our lure every second or two between turns on the reel. This method was successful; we caught several good-sized Pollack by the time dawn broke fully upon us. Then, the bait fish being gone, the Pollack sounded and our fishing was over for the day, since the Pollack would not return until dusk.

Our next fishing expedition was early in December when, warmly clad, my two friends and I drove to a breakwater where I felt the Pollack would be found. They were there, breaking water about two hundred feet offshore, too far for us to reach them with bait casting rods and the wood-bucktail-trailer lure. Fortunately we had included surf casting rods in our equipment but, with a steady breeze blowing into our faces, we still were unable to cast. We had promised some of our neighbors fresh fish (never do that) so we *had* to make good. After a short conference we discarded the wood lure and changed to a metal jig with a feather trailer and found that with this heavier rig we could reach them. Casting, we let the jig sink down some five to ten feet before commencing to reel in. We retrieved very slowly and were successful in catching nine Pollack, all of the large size, enough to satisfy ourselves and our hungry neighbors.

BOAT FISHING FOR POLLACK

At the time of year when surf casting is good for Pollack they are also offshore, seldom missing a day without surfacing. So boat fishing is in order. The best boat fishing is by trolling for them at high flood tide. Use an American or Japanese feather lure with a piece of squid or pork rind attached. Troll very slowly and let the line out from fifty to a hundred feet behind the boat. The line should be 36 pound test on a 200 yard reel. A 12 inch gut leader is generally used but, if you wish added weight to bring the lure lower in the water, use a five foot wire leader. Should more weight be desired a 2 to 4 ounce sinker can be added, generally with good results.

As you troll, lift the rod tip and lower it through an arc of about 3 feet. Do this continuously and keep on the alert, for when the Pollack hits, he hooks himself and then immediately trys to break free by coming violently to the surface. Failing in this maneuver, he will sink like a plummet to the bottom. Using these tactics, a twenty to thirty pound Pollack will provide a real tussel; the angler will welcome a little rest once the fish is boated. If too taut a line is held, the fish will probably break it. Once hooked the Pollack is not easily lost from the hook.

When bottom fishing for Pollack use squid or sea clams for bait on a 5/0 hook with three-way swivel and a 1 to 3 foot leader and a sinker of from 2 to 8 ounces in weight. Some fishermen will disagree in regards to the short leader, but I've yet to discover that this makes any difference. What *does* matter is the manner in which the hook is baited. Pains should be taken in preparing the bait; cut it in the same manner as for Cod fish i.e. into strips triangular in shape and from 3 to 8 inches long, 1½ to 2 inch base.

Codfish and Pollack are frequently found together because they like the same food, and Pollack, I've discovered, are as fond of the inside of a squid as are the Cod. If you've a mind to fish for Pollack and Cod at the same time there are two good methods for rigging the hooks. But first establish bottom by letting out the line until the sinker rests on the bottom and then take seven full turns on the reel. Fish at about this depth.

Now as to hooks. Using a 18 to 24 inch leader, one method is to place the first hook about 8 inches above the sinker; this hook is for Cod. Then place the second hook about a foot higher than the first, this one for Pollack. When you reel in, this top hook will, of course, strike the tip top guide, but there will be only about two feet of line (the distance from the top hook to the lower hook to the sinker) that will be dangling from the end of the rod tip. This length of line is easily handled.

The second method is to place the Cod hook as before—8

inches above the sinker—and then place the hook intended for Pollack above the Cod hook and about 6 feet from the bottom. The disadvantage of this arrangement is that, when the line is reeled in, the higher hook will hit the end of the rod tip and there will be over six feet of line dangling which must be pulled in by hand. Should two fish be hooked at the same time, six feet of dangling line with the struggling fish thereon will provide a most interesting problem for the angler.

Off Block Island, Pollack are often caught with a short leader and the hook set close to the sinker: from 2 to 10 inches above it. The rod for bottom fishing should be a 5 to 6 foot boat rod with a 150 to 200 yard reel of 36 to 45 pound test line. The leader should be of wire, gut or nylon and the sinkers, depending on the action of the water, should weigh from 3 to 10 ounces.

Dr. and Mrs. Walter H. Potter of Providence are ardent fishermen who enjoy fishing not only with their intimates but with casual acquaintances as well. Often, when fishing with comparative strangers, the fun-loving doctor would conceal from them the bait he was using, laughing off inquiries as he caught fish while his companions were having poor success.

"It's all in the know-how, folks," he'd chortle. "Just watch how I handle my line; keep an eye on my retrieve."

He would misdirect their attention until his fellow anglers gave up trying to detect anything unusual in his technique. Then when they had reached the point where they had about decided to give up fishing in favor of squat-tag, he would put them wise.

"It's not any special skill with the rod and reel, folks," he'd say. "It's the bait I'm using, the best bait for this particular fish. Then, I keep it *constantly fresh* on my hook. I'll bet I use twice as much bait as any of you. Something else you didn't notice is that my bait is the inside of the squid. Try it folks."

They would, and generally with gratifying results.

POMPANO   WEIGHT: Average 2 to 3 lbs.
Trachinotus carolinus   Record—30 lbs.
Family: *Carangidae*

Of the five species of Pompano ranging the eastern coastal waters of the United States, the largest species is found off the coast of Florida. This large species is caught by rod and reel, usually by trolling. A beautiful, nervous fish, it is reluctant to take a lure, but it hits hard and, once hooked, puts up a strong fight.

Many people consider the Pompano the finest food fish to be found in either the ocean or the rivers.

A school fish, the Pompano spends most of the time outside of bays, swimming well below the surface of the water. At high tide, the schools come inshore to search for shell fish,

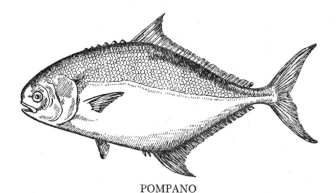

POMPANO

feeding freely during the last two hours of the incoming tide. When the school enters a bay, it breaks up, each fish going his own way.

Sand fleas and shrimp are considered the best bait for the beginner or average fisherman to use; the expert generally uses small feathers for either casting or trolling. Tackle recommended for it is a light boat rod, 100 to 150 yard reel of 15 to 30 pound test line, an 18 inch leader of nylon, gut or steel wire cable.

It is difficult to pin-point the localities in which this fish will be found because it does not, as some other species of fish, seem to follow any set pattern in its comings and goings.

On one of my visits to Palm Beach, Florida, I was invited to go Pompano fishing by Tony Accetta, an outstanding fisherman in those parts. We left Riviera Beach in Tony's fourteen foot, inboard motor boat, making our way down the Canal in the neighborhood of Palm Beach. We were after the smaller species of Pompano. We each had 20 pound test lines, 100 yard reels, and feathers Tony had manufactured. He had a 5 foot, 6 ounce Calcutta rod; I had my beryllium bait casting rod.

We started to fish and I soon discovered I was in for a fishing lesson; Tony caught fish while I did not. An excellent host, he tried to ease my feelings saying he thought my rod was too whippy. But I knew differently. He was successful because of the wrist snap he employed. Just two of us, we had room to manipulate the rod sideways and Tony had the knack of jumping his feather under the water in just the way that appealed to the fish. This wrist snap is the secret of catching Pompano, but, try as I might, I could not get the hang of it. Most of the anglers in those parts have mastered it; it is little known in the North. At the end of the day Tony had twelve nice fish; I, to my disgust, but one.

When trolling, use a fast wrist snap, either vertically or horizontally, jumping the lure and then letting it fall back, and repeat. As a rule, the Pompano takes the lure on the drop back, occasionally as it darts away from him. On the drop back the lure acts like a fish that is tired.

Difficult as this fish is to catch, it puts up a fight well out of proportion to its one pound weight. And being delicious to eat, it is well worth angling for.

Next year I want to go after the Great Pompano, or Permit, which averages about three feet in length and reaches the weight of twenty-seven pounds or more. This fellow should provide a lot of fun.

PORGY (SCUP)   WEIGHT: Average ¾ to 3 lbs.
Stenotomus chrysops   Record—5 lbs.
Family: *Sparidae*

The Porgy ranges from Maine southward all along the Atlantic coast. It is particularly abundant in southeast waters. It is a very prolific fish, the female discharging about a million ova during the breeding season. The young have a silvery body with bars which fade as they attain the adult stage when the skin becomes a darker grayish shade and the bars dark gray stripes. The Porgy has very sharp, spiny fins. It is highly prized as a food fish.

While the commercial catch of this fish runs into millions of pounds yearly, the casualities are quickly replaced by millions more, so there is no marked decrease in their numbers.

May to October is the fishing season for Porgy, and throughout the summer and fall porgy boats and open boats drift back and forth over the fishing grounds, literally covering their decks with Porgies. The fish caught at sea weigh from one to three pounds; those "inside", average less than a pound. They bite best at slack tide and during the incoming tide. Bottom feeders, they can be found over shellfish beds, sandy bottoms, around wrecks, reefs and in bays.

The Porgy seems to take one bait as well as another: shedder crabs, shrimp, worms, skimmers, small pieces of squid

PORGY

and soft shell clams. Skimmers, being plentiful, are the favorite bait with fishermen.

While the boats outside are very busy, the rowboat fisherman can also enjoy catching the smaller Porgies in the bays. He should use a 5 to 10 ounce overall 6 foot rod with a 100 yard reel of 20 to 36 pound test line with a 2 to 5 ounce sinker, 2/0 to 4/0 O'Shaughnessy hooks with a 3 foot stainless steel or gut leader.

The Porgy snaps at the bait, taking a very firm hold, but, since they have very small mouths, the bait must be small so that it can be easily swallowed. They offer firm resistance to being boated by turning broadside and counter-wise to the pull of the line, thus using the water to aid them in their fight for freedom.

The fishing technique employed for catching Porgies is to first establish bottom and then, having let down your line, give quick, little jerks to the rod tip, up and down, being careful that the bait does not rise higher than about a foot from the bottom. Do not jerk the rod swiftly.

The Porgy has a very sharp dorsal fin which can inflict a wound that will be quite painful for a considerable length of time. Before trying to remove the hook, slide the hand along the top of the fish's head towards the tail, smoothing down and firmly holding the dorsal fin. Be certain of a strong grip before removing the hook.

I was once engaged by a Mr. Blank to take him and his nephew out for Porgies. It seems that the gentleman was very anxious to make a fisherman out of the boy who was about thirteen years old, and who seemed most reluctant to go. We drove to a bay, procured a boat and some bait and I rowed them out to a spot where I felt there would be fish. On the way Mr. Blank informed me that all he required of me was to take them to good fishing grounds; that he was something of an expert and that he would do all the instructing of the boy. We reached our spot and I sat back to watch proceedings.

Mr. Blank had the proper tackle, but I soon saw he had little knowledge in regards to catching Porgies. He jerked his line up and down so fast that the fish would have had to have been a sprinter to catch up with it and he put on bait far too large for the fish's mouth. Seated in the stern he kept calling instructions, all wrong, to his nephew in the bow. The nephew dutifully, if sullenly, followed the tutoring, neither getting any fish. After about an hour, Mr. Blank decided to change seats. Making his way to the bow, he jostled the boy, trying to pass him, so that the boy's rod dropped overboard. I grabbed it as it went under. Mr. Blank expressed his opinion of the boy's clumsiness and squatted in the bow; his nephew settled in the stern and lost interest in fishing.

How he caught it, I'll never know but, suddenly, with a whoop, Mr. Blank yanked his rod into the air, swung around, and slapped me in the face with a half pound Porgy. I brushed off his apology and he returned enthusiastically to his fishing.

A half hour passed and Mr. B. decided to change seats again. This was accomplished with a minor casualty; he stepped on my hand as I was trying to balance the boat. He settled himself in the stern and his nephew draped himself over the bow, rod propped under him, looking longingly at the distant shore.

Another half-hour and Mr. Blank, making remarks under his breath concerning my ability to find a good spot, decided that, since he was getting no fish, he would demonstrate to his nephew how to cast. The boy watched for a moment or two then turned his attention again to the shore, just at the moment when, with a grand flourish, Mr. Blank essayed a side arm cast. He lost control of the line on the back motion, the lure whizzed by my face and hooked his nephew in the seat of his pants. That did it. I couldn't help making a few very pertinent remarks about the danger of a lure flying through the air and how one, who is not proficient, should be smart enough to take some advice from one who knows. Naturally, Mr. Blank took offense.

I never saw Mr. Blank and his nephew again. The boy was very happy to get back to land and somehow, I've the notion that he never grew up to be a fisherman.

SAILFISH (ATLANTIC) WEIGHT: Average 35 to 50 lbs.
Istiophorus americanus Record—123 lbs.
Family: *Istiophoridae*

SAILFISH

The largest species of Sailfish is in the Pacific but the Atlantic species is more colorful. The huge dorsal fin, or sail, is a lavender hue, darker purple at the tips, and it is dotted with small purple spots. The back is a deep blue; the belly and lower sides a silvery white and in the center is a bright green stripe. Blue dots give the effect of vertical lines along the sides. The tip of the elongated upper lip, or bill, is a dark purple and blue where it joins the head.

When swimming in the water, the sail can be tucked back into a slot on the back and the ventral and pectoral fins press against the body thus giving the fish a streamlined form. It has a powerful tail that is crescent in shape.

The sail, apparently, is only raised when the fish is frightened or aroused and exactly what its function is has not been determined. It is possibly used as a brake in landing, after a jump of some forty feet across the water or, again, it may serve as a sense organ as the fish lies with it outstretched on the surface of the water.

The Sailfish is probably the fastest swimming fish in the ocean; it can cover a hundred yards in about three seconds. A shy fish, it is difficult to hook and unless the bait is very fresh it will drop it. When hooked, the Sailfish strikes out, going into an acrobatic dance, frequently standing almost vertically on the surface of the water in his effort to shake the hook from his mouth. A beautiful sight to see. However, it does not have the stamina that the related swordfish and marlin possess. But, like these fish, it will on occasion, attack the boat in its frenzy.

It is uncertain just where the Sailfish breeds but it is probably in the vicinity of the Florida coast. The female is fatter and much heavier than the male and not as strenuous a fighter.

When the Sailfish strikes, he first mauls the bait with his bill to either maim or stun it. He then closes on it, turning it over in the process of swallowing it. So, before setting the hook, time must be allowed after he strikes with his bill to permit him to swallow the bait. I discovered that a medium fast count of ten is adequate. However, this rule is not infallible because of the variance in the speed in counting induced by the excitement of having a Sailfish on the line. A fisherman would have to be utterly without emotion not to get excited, and as for the beginner, well, it will be very difficult for him to count at all, let alone in a calm and exact manner.

Trolling from charter boats is the generally accepted way in which to go out for this fish. Light tackle should be used and, if not fishing with outriggers, fish with the reel in free spool, allowing the line to drop back on the initial strike. For tackle use a boat rod with a 6 ounce tip, a 45 pound test line, 200 to 400 yard reel, 8/0 to 10/0 hooks and a 15 foot leader of piano wire. Mullet is a popular bait.

Don't let rough water stop you from going out. During the winter months the best fishing is usually when a norther is blowing.

This fish can be taken off the coast of Florida any month in the year. Sailfish are, in the main, caught for the sport of it, they are not the most edible of fish so, unless wanted as a trophy, cut it loose once you have made the catch. He will return to the water to live and fight another day, furnishing a thrill for some other angler. That is unless he has been hooked through the eye or stomach when the chances are slim for survival. The practice of releasing the fish is very much in vogue; over eighty per cent of those now being caught are being set free.

I do not know of anyone who has tried using a plug covered with an eel skin for a lure. I've a hunch this rig would attract the Sailfish more readily than the whole bait fish generally used. The bait fish, when trolled, is inclined to roll in the water; the plug would ride straight, like a fish swimming. The next time I go to Florida I am going to experiment with this lure.

For the average fisherman, charter boats are expensive, so he hopes to realize on his investment by catching a fish. A beginner, after trolling a reasonable length of time and no fish, will be smart to permit the captain of the boat to follow a certain procedure. The captain, knowing the technique of hooking the fish, will hook one and then turn the rod over to the anxious angler, and he's on his own. This method is good for the novice, for by paying close attention to the captain, he can learn something, probably catch his fish, and the captain benefits for he can fly his flag signifying a catch.

If you cannot afford to charter a boat but have access to a small private boat, and you are new at the game, there is no law against your following, at a respectful distance, in the wake of a charter boat. The charter boat is going to the best fishing grounds, so tag along observing where it is going, how fast it is travelling, and, when a Sailfish is hooked, how it is handled. This is an inexpensive way to gain knowledge by observation.

If you should happen to be alone and wish to go fishing for Sailfish in a charter boat, seek out the fleet and frequently you can join a boat that is making up a party, paying your share of expenses.

When going after your first Sailfish, either in private or party boat, remember that you can see him hit the bait and then follow up to swallow it. Realizing this element of time in his process of taking the bait should help you to keep calm, and, if you can do so, you should hook your fish. If after the

initial strike and drop back of the line you find the fish isn't
on, reel in fast. He will probably follow and take the bait.

SHAD (AMERICAN)   WEIGHT: Average 4 lbs.
Alosa sapidissima   Record—14 lbs.
Family: *Clupeidae*

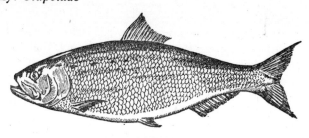

SHAD

When America was still the Colonies, the Shad, largest
member of the Herring family, was so abundant that, in the
spring, its numbers choked the mouths of rivers and streams—
masses of fish swimming to headwaters to spawn. For, like the
Salmon, the Shad migrates from the sea to the rivers during
this season in order to reproduce. The female, heavier than the
male, will deposit from thirty thousand to one hundred and
fifty thousand eggs when spawning. These eggs hatch in from
six to ten days time and, within six months, the young attain
the length of about three inches. Maturity is reached in three
to four years.

The Shad is not as abundant as of yore due to the destruc-
tion caused by industrial pollution and also to its having been
caught in great numbers over a period of years. At the turn of
the century the Federal government found it necessary to take
steps to prevent the extinction of the species. Today the Shad
is most abundant along the coast line from North Carolina to
Long Island and in the Hudson river roughly two million pounds
of Shad are caught each spring.

It is good sport catching Shad, for they fight hard, twisting
about when hooked and leaping from the water as they try
to shake the hook from their mouths. Frequently, unless the
angler is very alert, this manoeuver will be successful. The
fisherman must keep the line constantly taut and the rod tip
elevated to prevent the fish shaking the hook from his mouth.

Should the angler be fishing an inlet, he will be most successful if he casts across the tide flow and retrieves slowly, stopping his lure every few seconds, then taking a few turns on the reel, and then repeating the operation as he reels in.

Night fishing spots for Shad are not too numerous, so it is advisable to inquire at a local tackle shop as to the best place to go and the proper lure to use. The tackle shop owner, being on the scene, is generally acquainted with local fishing conditions; follow his advice.

The tackle recommended for American Shad is: fly rod or bait casting rod, with a 100 to 200 yard reel of 20 pound test line, gut or nylon leader 12 to 18 inches long, 2/0 to 4/0 hooks. Or a Spinning rod with momofilament line, 100 to 200 yards. Use lures such as small feathers or spinners.

The Hickory Shad *(Polombus mediosroc)*, a sub member of the Herring family, ranges from Florida to Maine. Smaller than the American Shad—averaging two to three pounds—it can be readily seen from shore as it chases bait during June and July and again during September and October. Their silvery bodies flash brilliantly in the sunlight as they skin the surafce.

The same tackle that is used for the American Shad is used for the Hickory. However, if wanted for bait, use un-baited triple hooks and snag or jig them. Once caught, hook one through the dorsal fin, close to the back, and it will make an excellent bait for the Striped Bass that are generally lurking a few hundred yards away, waiting to make a meal of the Hickories. Do *not* hook the Hickory down into its back; it will die, and a dead fish has no attraction for the Stripers.

SHARKS   WEIGHT: Depends on the species, 10 to 25,000
              pounds.
              Record catch, angling—1,919 lbs.

There are forty-seven species and sub-species of Shark inhabiting our coastal waters. Not all Sharks are predatory despite many stories to the contrary.

The Shark does not have scales, his body being covered with a tough hide that is studded with denticles, small tooth-like formations that give the hide an abrasive quality.

Sharks, in general, lay eggs, although few in comparison to other species of fish. These eggs have a large yolk from which the embryo draws nourishment for a considerable length of time and is thus able to care for itself as soon as it is hatched. However, in some species, the egg is hatched within the mother, the young being nourished by a growth extending from the region of her gills.

THE WHALE SHARK *(Rhineodon typicus)*

This Shark is the largest of living fish; it is next to the mammal whales in size. It is found in all the warm waters of the Atlantic and Pacific, off the Cape of Good Hope, the West Indies and in the Mediterranean. It has a checkerboard

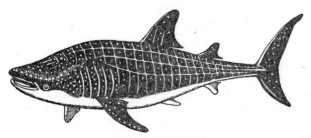

WHALE SHARK

pattern formation of lines on its back, dotted with whitish spots, which distinguishes it from the Basking Shark that approaches it in size. Harmless, it possesses small teeth about an eighth of an inch long, some three thousand to each jaw. They feed on small marine animals and put up a strenuous fight when harpooned. It is known to reach 25,000 pounds in weight.

THE BASKING SHARK *(Cetorhinus maximus)*

Next in size and weight to the Whale Shark, the Basking Shark reaches a length of some forty-five feet. It obtained its name from its habit of lolling and basking in the sun on the surface of the ocean, alternately exposing its belly and sides to the sun's rays. Despite its huge size, this Shark is quiet and inoffensive. It has small teeth that are wholly inadequate to a predatory career but they serve admirably to break up the tiny crustaceans, copepods and similar marine foods on which it subsists. The liver of the Basking Shark will yield about two hundred gallons of oil, and for this reason it was the earlier days greatly sought after by fishing fleets out of New Bedford and vicinity. Now rare, it is still hunted off the coasts of Iceland and Ireland.

The Mackerel Shark (*Lamna nasus*)

One member of the Mackerel Shark family is the Blue Shark or Porbeagle (*Lamna cornubia*). This fish, heavy shouldered and sea-blue in color, reaches a length of about twelve feet, and it gives birth to live young. While it prefers warm seas it ranges as far north as Nova Scotia. It is a nuisance to fisherman's nets and it destroys numerous schools of hake, menhaden, herring, shad and other fish.

Another member of the family is the White Shark or Man-eater. It (*Carcharodon carcharias*) is the largest of the Mackerel Sharks growing to between thirty and forty feet in length. In color it is black, slaty gray, lead white, with large triangular teeth with sharp cutting edges. Ranging the warm temperate waters, it is the only Shark reputed to attack man. Occasionally it is found as far north as the waters off eastern Nova Scotia. The food of the Mackerel Shark consists mainly of sea turtles and large fish.

The Hammerhead Shark (*Sphyrna zygaena*)

The strange formation of the head of this fish enables it to use its head as a rudder when making sharp turns in pursuit of its prey. The Hammerhead, swimming with dorsal and caudal fins above the surface of the water, is of the high seas and it is found in tropical waters around the globe. Due to elongated nostrils which are situated along the edge of the "hammer" it has a remarkable sense of smell and is able to scent blood, spilled far out at sea. Because of this ability, it is generally the first Shark to arrive on the scene to survey the situation with bulging eyes.

The Hammerhead averages about twelve feet in length but is known to achieve some seventeen feet. A large member of this species will weigh three-quarters of a ton. Its food consists of sea clams, fish and barnacles. The female produces large families, thirty-seven young having been found in one mother on one occasion.

The Thresher Shark (*Alopias vulpinus*)

The long, scythe-shaped tail of this fish is designed for a special function; it is used to flail porpoises to death and to herd schools of fish. Working in pairs, the Thresher Sharks, flailing their tails about, will force a school of menhaden or herring into a compact group so as to feed on them with greater convenience.

This Shark is from fifteen to twenty feet long and is found in all temperate waters, ranging in the Atlantic, as far north as Block Island and occasionally to the Gulf of the St. Lawrence. It is a nuisance to fishermen, tearing or tangling their nets and driving away the schools of fish it does not decimate.

THE TIGER SHARK *(Galeocerdo cuvier)*

The Tiger Shark has a large head of massive construction; a convex snout that overhangs wide jaws set with strong teeth shaped like a sickle. Its habitat is the high seas of the tropics but an occasional straggler has been found as far north as Maine waters. While, authentically, it has not been know to attack man, it is greatly feared by the natives of the West Indies.

This Shark averages some twelve feet in length but has been known to have attained the length of thirty feet. It preys on sea turtles; fishes and on other Sharks.

THE SAND SHARK *(Carcharias tanrus)*

With the exception of the Dogfish, the Sand Shark is the most common of the Shark family. They are found between the Bay of Funday and Cape Cod and down along the New England coast. During the warm months they swim close to the shore and into the mouths of rivers, but when cold weather sets in they depart for southern waters. A sluggish fish, swimming leisurely along, dorsal fins and tails protruding above the surface of the water, they can, when the occasion arises, quickly summon sufficient energy to enable them to surround and decimate a school of Bluefish. They also destroy large numbers of menhaden, alewife, flounder, butterfish and cunner,

The full grown adult is about six feet in length and weighs three to four hundred pounds. The color is gray spotted with brown with the fin occasionally being edged with black.

The Sand Shark migrates during the months of July and August, feeding along the Atlantic shoreline from the full moon in July until the full moon in August.

For the fisherman who cannot afford the time nor expense involved in boat fishing for Tuna or other large game fish that are caught out in deep water, I recommend shore fishing for Sand Shark. Hooked from shore, a three hundred pound Shark will provide as much of a thrill as would hooking a large game fish offshore in a boat. For Mr. Shark when caught, will strip three to four hundred yards of line from the reel with great rapidity. Some fish when they strike, will jump from the water; others will run a short distance with the line, but the Shark immediately takes off for distant waters.

When you have hooked a Shark and he is speeding away with your line, do not touch the line as it pays out. It is running off the reel at such a high rate of speed that, touched, it will cut a finger to the bone. Even a light pressure will produce a severe burn. After you have landed the Shark, be very careful to keep out of the way of its tail as it thrashes about. A blow from the tail of a Shark weighing one hundred and fifty pounds or more can easily break a leg; smaller Sharks, while capable of delivering a severe blow, do not have the strength to do any real damage.

It is always advisable to chum when shore fishing for this fish, menhaden having the preference with mackerel a second choice. The menhaden can be either fresh or frozen and about a half bushel should be prepared at a time. Although any fish chum will attract Sharks, they can scent menhaden at a greater distance than any other chum employed. To prepare menhaden for chum use either a meat grinder, small hand axe or a sharp knife and render it into small bits. Chum with the outgoing tide in deep water off a beach near an inlet or off a rocky formation or jetty.

Sharks can be fished for both day and night, but generally night fishing is the best. Once you have tied into a Shark of any decent size, be prepared for a battle of from one to three hours, for you will find that he is a stubborn fighter and difficult to land.

Many a fisherman has hooked a sizeable Bass and, as he was reeling in, has had a Shark swoop down and deprive him of his catch. To add insult to injury the Shark generally snaps off all but the head of the fish thus affording the angler the dubious pleasure of trying to figure out the size of the fish stolen from him, estimating its weight from the size of the head remaining on his line. Such occurrences have been responsible for many lurid cuss words being added to the vocabulary of the angler.

When boat fishing for Shark the fish is generally shot with a .22 pistol as it is brought along side, then a stout rope looped around the tail enables the fisherman to boat it.

Shark tackle should be a heavy surf or boat rod with a 400 to 600 yard reel, 45 pound test line and hooks not less than 9/0 to 12/0, if anything, larger. The leader should be a 15 foot stainless steel cable or piano wire. The bait used is a whole fish, menhaden or mackerel.

THE MAKO SHARK (Isurus glaucus)

"Mako", in the language of the Maoris of New Zealand means shark. Ranging from New Zealand to Cuban waters, it is found farther north in Atlantic waters, as far as New Jersey. The only game fish of the Shark family, it is fished for extensively from charter boats.

The Mako attains a weight of 800 pounds and is a difficult fish to land with rod and line, for on being brought along side the boat for gaffing, it will, calling on reserve power, try to attack its tormentors, putting up a terrific fight.

The tackle recommended for the Mako is a 6 foot overall boat rod of glass or beryllium copper with 36 ounce tip, 18 to 20 inch butt, 800 to 1600 yard reel of 117 to 216 pound test line, 10/0 to 14/0 Sobey hooks and stainless steel cable or wire leader 15 feet long. The bait is menhaden, mackerel, whiting and herring.

Two fishing pals of mine, Wicky and Marty, had been after me for some time to take them out Mako fishing. They had never been in a charter boat party due to circumstances. Either they hadn't had the time when party boats were being made up, or when at leisure they'd been unable to find others to go along, thus reducing the expense which for the two alone was a bit steep for their pocket books. So, Wicky in particular, hipped on the idea of catching a Mako, had pestered me to the point where, good friend though he was, he was fast becoming a bore. I just could not brush him off, so, one day, taking Marty into my confidence, I planned to cure him of pestering me.

Captain Morse, a commercial fishing friend of mine owned a boat but it was not equipped, as are charter boats, with the proper tackle. I took Marty into my confidence, then contacted the Captain, told him my plan. One hot day in July he telephoned me that the Mako were running and now was the time to go after them.

I phoned Wicky and Marty and they came to my tackle shop the next day, Wicky bubbling over; Marty anxious to see the fun. I provided Wicky with an old hickory rod with a 20 ounce butt, 40 ounce tip, 300 yard 10/0 reel of 108 pound test line. The rod was adequate but the line was entirely too short for the sport at hand.

We drove to the dock, boarded the boat and soon reached the fishing grounds. Almost immediately we saw two Makos swimming along side the boat. I judged them to weigh 200 and 400 pounds, respectively. Telling Wicky I'd start him right, I took his rod, watched my chance and dropped the bait in front of the big one. He took the bait and quickly I handed the rod to Wicky telling him to hold the Mako tight because of the short length of the line. Then I joined Marty to watch the action.

Highly excited, Wicky held the line as taut as he could, the fight was even for a few minutes and then the Shark took some extra line. Wicky shifted his grip and, coming in contact with the running line, got a severe burn on his fingers. Cussing, he held on while Marty and I threw pails of water to cool off angler, hands and reel. For a half hour Wicky pulled, pumped and sweated; pumped, pulled and cussed. He would have long since lost the Mako if the Captain had not maneuvered the boat to aid him. Then Wicky called to me for aid. "Sorry, old boy, I can't help you, it wouldn't be sporting," I said. "Besides, you've got your Mako on; stick with it." Finally, after forty-five minutes of extreme effort on Wicky's part, the Mako was brought along side and, not wishing to boat him, the Captain killed it with several well-placed shots.

Wicky sank into a deck chair, exhausted. "Jerry," he said, "I think there's something fishy about this. How come you gave me such a short line? Well, I caught him but if I can't have a bigger reel next time, I'm going to settle for a three-pound Striper. I'm pooped out."

He never pestered me again to go out for Mako.

THE DOGFISH SHARK

In the spring two species of this fish infest the New England coastal waters, the smooth Dogfish *(Cynias Canis)* and the spiny Dogfish *(Squalus acanthias)*. These small Sharks hunt in schools, attacking cod, mackerel, haddock and herring, killing or driving them away. They are a nuisance to fishermen, tearing nets and stealing fish from hooks. The damage they do, yearly, to tackle and gear is estimated to run into hundreds of thousands of dollars.

The spiny Dodfish has a sharp spike, placed just in front of each dorsal fin, that can inflict a severe wound if the fish is seized.

It has been reported that the Dogfish attacks swimmers but this has never been authentically substantiated.

THE NURSE SHARK *(Ginglymostoma cirratum)*

This harmless fish is seldom found north of the waters off the Carolinas. Off the Florida Keys it comes into shallow water to mate and it is reputed that boys, discovering its presence by its high protruding fin, will mount this sluggish swimmer and, holding on by the pectoral fins, will ride the confused fish until reaching deep water.

This Shark averages from six to ten feet in length and feeds mainly on squid and shrimp. The female retains her eggs within the body during the whole period of incubation, producing the young alive. When the young are born they have a spattering of brown spots that disappear when they reach the adult stage.

Three other species of the better known Sharks are the Dusky Shark *(Carcharhinus obscurus),* the Blue Shark *(Prionace glauca)* and the Brown Shark *(Carcharhinus milberti).* They are all harmless to man.

A word about shore fishing with a fifteen foot leader. A leader of this length is necessary because a shorter one can easily be severed by the abrasive skin of the Shark as he rolls and turns over to seize the bait. The angler cannot cast a fifteen foot leader as he would a regular surf rig, therefore he must throw it out as he would a hand line.

An adequate, inexpensive outfit is a 6 to 8 foot Calcutta bamboo rod with a tip top guide No. 20, two or three side guides No. 18 spaced evenly down the rod from the tip top guide to the butt.

SNAPPER BLUES   LENGTH: Average 6 to 8 in.
(Pomatomus saltatrix)   Record: None

The name "Snapper" is usually given to the young of the Bluefish. They average from six to eight inches in length.

About the beginning of August the Snapper Blues come into the inlets and bays to remain until October. They swim in on the tide, feed until it turns, swim out and then repeat the performance. The best places to fish for them is under docks and bridges and around causeways. Use either a fly rod of 4 to 6 ounces or a bait casting rod of from 4 to 6 feet long, a 100 yard reel with 10 to 20 pound test line and Snapper hooks. These hooks are made especially for this fish having a long shank, about 4 inches. This length prevents the leader being severed by the Snapper, something it is apt to do, as it has very sharp teeth. If the tide is running strongly use split shot sinkers on the line.

If fishing an inlet or bay where there are several bridges, start your casting from the first bridge just as the tide commences to flow in under the bridge. As the bites lessen because the fish are moving on with the tide, reel in and proceed to the next bridge. Timed correctly, you should arrive there just as the tide comes in full under it and the fish will be feeding. Repeat this performance until you have exhausted all the bridges in the inlet or bay. Such a procedure is good for both incoming and outgoing tides.

The Snapper Blue, despite his small size, affords good sport when fished for with a fly rod; they swim fast and fight hard when hooked.

During their fall migration in October they can be seen close in along the shore of the ocean. Cast with a block tin jig or a feather and a piece of wood. This wood is about five inches long and weighs from 1 to 4 ounces. If using feathers be certain to be provided with plenty of them as the Snapper Blue can chew them up with great rapidity. A fast retrieve has been proved to be the best method to use to catch this fish.

One day late in September, a man, his wife and daughter came to me. Almost tearfully the wife explained that they were beginners, that they had been out a number of times and had not been able to catch a fish, *any* kind of fish. I noted their tackle; it was suitable for Snapper Blues, so, having some time on my hands, I volunteered to see that they caught some fish. We went to an inlet that had two bridges and I knew Snappers would be there. We arrived just as the tide was beginning to come in but I took time to demonstrate and explain the proper method of casting and retrieving. I did not fish, spending the next half-hour giving helpful tips, and suddenly all three of them had a fish on the line. I never have met more enthusiastic anglers.

Following the tide, we went on to the next bridge. Here,

having become a bit more proficient in handling rod and reel, they caught a respectable mess of Snappers. And that evening three very tired but happy fishermen made their way homeward after showering me with thanks.

The most commonly used bait for Snapper Blues is the Silversides (Salt-water minnow, Shiner, Sperling) a small fish of from 2 to 4 inches in length. To properly place it on the hook, pierce one eye and then push the hook on through the other eye. Then push the barb of the hook into the back just back of the dorsal fin and force the hook on through the body so that the whole hook comes out on the side from which the operation started.

TARPON (SILVER KING)   WEIGHT: Average 30 to
Tarpon atlanticus   80 lbs.
Family: *Culpeidae*   Record—an-
                                              gling, 247 lbs.

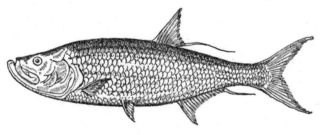

TARPON

Anglers consider catching Tarpon, the original game fish, the sport of sports. The Tarpon range from off the Carolinas southward to Florida and Texas. While occasional stragglers are found as far north as Cape Cod, it is the misfortune of northern fishermen that this fish is not plentiful in northern waters.

The Tarpon has a protruding lower jaw, soft-rayed fins, forked tail and depressible dorsal and anal fins. Its eyes, with dilated pupils, are set in armor-plated sockets calculated to resist the pressure of two hundred fathoms. Its body is covered with large scales three or four inches in diameter that reflect with a metallic sheen. Known as the "Silver King" it travels far up rivers in search of food, being able to live in brackish, muddy water as readily as in salt water. It likes to lie in wait for food in channels and it frequents inlets, bays and lagoons. Where this fish spawns has not as yet been determined. One theory is that it spawns in the rivers of Florida's west coast. Another that it spawns in the open sea near the coast. This theory is based on the premise that the young pass through a larval stage before becoming fish. After hatching, it is believed the young fry seek inland waters and they are the length of about a foot by the end of the first year. In maturity the Tarpon averages from four to five feet in length and attains an outside weight of three hundred pounds. A female has been known to lay as many as ten million eggs in a spawning season. The female of the species is larger than the male but not as active. Essentially a warm water fish, the Tarpon is sensitive to change and when the water temperature drops it seeks warmer regions.

The majority of Tarpon caught weigh from 30 to 80 pounds but many are boated weighing up to 170 pounds; a 200 pounder is a rarity. It is known there are bigger ones but where these members of the species keep themselves is a mystery.

Tarpon are fished for from boat and from shore. The tackle used is bait casting rods, surf rods and fly rods. When trolling from a boat, do it at a slow pace, passing back and forth over the area where the fish are known to be, fishing with bait casting rod and small plugs or feathers for lures.

When still fishing from a boat, the hook is baited with crab, shrimp or cut bait and the line is lowered to the bottom. Time should be allowed to permit the fish to take and swallow the bait, before setting the hook. The favorite food of the Tarpon is mullet but cutlass fish, shrimp, crabs and sea catfish also make excellent bait.

Surf fishing requires a surf rod with feathers and plugs heavy enough to cast. Should additional weight be needed, the Sylvester wood float can be added to the lighter lure.

Small Tarpon can be fished for the year round in small bays and rivers using a fly rod with streamer flies or small plugs. Again remember to allow the fish time to swallow the hook. The Tarpon has a hard lining in its mouth and time is required so that the hook will penetrate deeply, thus off-setting the chances of the fish shaking free as he goes into his acrobatics.

When a Tarpon is hooked, he almost invariably emerges from the water with a rush, making leap after leap as high as fifteen feet, a silvery flash in the air, trying to rid himself of the hook. Due to the horny lining in its mouth which resists the penetration of the hook, seventy-five percent of those hooked are lost.

Since the Tarpon can span thirty feet of water in a leap, it is difficult to boat him with rod and reel. Skill and much effort are required to play the fish so as to tire him out far enough away from the boat so as to insure that one of his leaps does not carry him aboard. This has occurred and anything in the path of the fish has been shattered or knocked overboard. Fishermen have been known to have been slapped into the sea and drowned.

The majority of fishermen seek Florida waters for Tarpon and once having caught the fish, generally return it to the water. It is the sport of catching the Tarpon—a sport which can be dangerous—that attracts the angler. The flesh of this fish is not too edible although broiled, fried or baked, the flesh of the very young is tasty.

As to fishing technique, work the plug with a skip and jump, then at intervals let the lure lie on top of the water, barely moving it forward and then dropping it back. At times the Tarpon hits the jumping plug; at other times, the slowly moving lure. The phase of the moon, rip of the tide and cool weather affect the movement of the bait fish and, therefore, the feeding of the Tarpon and the manner in which he takes the bait. Many fishermen try to discover just what the Tarpon are feeding on but, personally, I prefer to find out the *manner* in which they are feeding: whether the bait fish are coming fast, slow or at medium speed. Once determined, this dictates the handling of my lure.

Plan your fishing vacation for the months of May and June when Tarpon fishing is excellent with the best time being during the full moon in May. However, the other months are all productive of good sport, also.

The most popular method used for Tarpon is to cast from a stationary boat, using a bait casting rod with small plugs or spinners for lures. They are also caught trolling with whole mullet for bait.

I do not believe the Tarpon deliberately attacks the boat of the fisherman who has hooked him. Most fish, when brought up for boating, give a last convulsive effort to free themselves, and then surrender. I believe the Tarpon loses all sense of direction as he is reeled in closer and closer to the boat, and, brought too close, one of his last frantic leaps is likely to carry him aboard.

On a recent trip to Florida, my friend Mike and I went out for some Tarpon bay fishing. We had hired a small boat and had light tackle with us: beryllium bait casting rods; level winding reels of 275 yards of 18 pound test nylon line and small plugs for lures.

It was a beautiful day and the mullet were there, and in the first few hours fishing Mike and I hooked and lost fifteen Tarpon weighing, we judged, from 25 to 100 pounds. Twice we had to hurriedly maneuver the boat to avoid being swamped by a leaping "Silver King." We had about decided it was not our day, having caught no fish, when, simultaneously, we both had a Tarpon on the line. Mike's fish was some distance farther out than mine and after a time he lost him. Meanwhile I'd been playing my fish, having a real battle but bringing him in closer and closer. Finally he began to falter, his leaps becoming less violent and less frequent. I applied pressure to bring him in and Mike chose that moment to lose his hat overboard. As he made a lunging grab for it the Tarpon with a tremendous leap landed amidships. It was fortunate for my companion he had shifted his position for the Tarpon hit at almost the exact spot where he had been sitting. As it was, the flailing tail knocked Mike overboard and, as he went, the Tarpon with a convulsive flop plopped back into the water.

Mike, spluttering, came to the surface and I instinctively set my drag and then helped him inboard. Meanwhile my fish had swum out about a hundred yards to stop and, apparently, view the rescue.

Once Mike was aboard I jumped to my rod and began pumping it; the fight was on again. The big fish leaped and leaped until I wondered if he would ever tire. But finally his exertions took their toll and I had my first Tarpon, a beauty that weighed forty-one pounds.

After this adventure Mike showed a marked lack of enthusiasm for Tarpon fishing. Try as I might I could not get him to go out again. "There are plenty of other fish," he would argue "why not go after them?" I tried to shame him into going for one more trip. Why should a little forty pound fish spoil our Tarpon fishing? Did he realize we had but three days left of our vacation? And also, the probability of such an incident occurring again was very remote.

"Look, Jerry," he said. "It ain't that Tarpon, it's what I saw when I went into the drink."

"Yea? A couple of mermaids I suppose."

"Mermaids!" he snorted. "If they were, they are the homliest old bags I ever saw anywhere. No, sir, not mermaids. Two crocodiles were waiting down there, grinning right in my face."

Well, we hadn't had a drink, s'help me and maybe he had a point; strange things *do* sometimes happen when fishing.

I missed out on my second Tarpon fishing expedition due to an unbearable, jumping toothache. Two days after the experience with Mike, Lee Masters of Clearwater, Florida, invited me to go out with him, but ardent fisherman that I am, that darned tooth forced me to decline.

Lee had his boat docked at Tarpon Springs, a considerable distance from Clearwater, and minus my company, he set out from the Springs. The full moon was just beginning to wane and the Tarpon were feeding freely. Lee missed several strikes and then hooked a big one. The fish gave a few gigantic leaps and then decided to go away from that place, towing Lee and his boat, willy-nilly behind him. He pulled the boat at high speed all the way to Clearwater where, passing under a bridge into the inlet, the line was severed on an abutment and the fish was lost.

I have always regretted that I missed being taken for that ride back home.

TAUTOG (BLACKFISH)   WEIGHT: Average 2 to
Tautog onitis   10 lbs.
Family: *Labridae*   Record—20
                                                   lbs.

The time to start out after the Tautog is on the new moon or the full moon in April. It is then that the Tautog begins to come in from deep water to spawn in the big bays and inlets. Occasionally they may be a bit late, but following some mysterious mandate of Nature, they are as a rule very punctual in arriving.

The Tautog is equipped with two sets of teeth, one set in the jaw proper, the other set is far back in the mouth. Using this array, the fish is able to crunch the hardest shell fish or crustacean.

Tautog are often called Blackfish but it is not, however, to be confused with the mamalian Blackfish—also called the Pilot Whale—which is of a much greater size and is a species of the small-toothed Whale.

Heavy tackle is needed for the Tautog for two reasons. First, the mouth of the fish is lined with a heavy membrane, which when it strikes, makes it necessary for the angler to apply considerable force when setting the hook so that the barb will penetrate. Again, the Tautog, when hooked, will almost invariably try to take refuge among rocks, and stout tackle is needed to prevent his doing so. Use a 6 foot overall boat rod

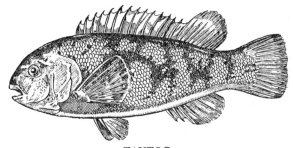

TAUTOG

with a 10 ounce tip, a 150 yard reel of 36 pound test line, number 3 tarred line snelled hook, 1 to 6 ounce sinker.

A light rod with a 20 pound test line *can* be used, but if the hook is set too hard, the line may break. And also, should the Tautog reach his sanctuary among the rocks, he cannot be horsed out with light tackle.

Early fishing for Tautog is done from rowboats or party boats and the best water in which to fish for them is over rocky ledges, among rocks, in weed and rock areas and over mussel bars. Don't look for them very far from these areas, for they constitute the natural habitat of the fish, affording him protection.

Some fishermen, in their ignorance, will spend hours casting away from a rocky formation and into a weed area that has a sandy bottom. If this weed area has no rocks, or a rocky ledge, their efforts will be rewarded merely with a catch of dogfish or skates. And frequently the bait is lost when reeling in, stripped from the hook by the weeds. So, fish close to rocks.

Often I've observed a Tautog swimming leisurely along the shore among rock-weed formations until he reached an open, sandy bottom. Here he would take off quickly across the exposed stretch and not slacken his pace until he reached the next rocky bottom or weed-rock bed. Then he would again resume his easy pace.

When surf fishing for Tautog early in the season, find a spot where there is either a mussel-bar or some rocks. Not necessarily a large number of rocks; a few will suffice to attract any Tautog that are in the vicinity. I've fished spots where only two or three rocks of any considerable size jutted up from the water and have caught a dozen Tautog on one tide, and then, returning six hours later to the spot, have enjoyed the same good fishing on the next tide.

One good feature of such a spot is that, although the Tautog and Bergalls (Cunners) are generally found together, here no Bergalls will be in evidence. The explanation is simple. Bergalls frequent spots where rocks are numerous; they shun places where they are scarce because, few in number, they do not afford the Bergalls any real protection from their enemies. So, at this place, I could use bloodworms, which are my favorite bait, and not have them stolen by thieving Bergalls, expert at stealing bait.

The Tautog is also adept at pilfering bait unless the angler is constantly on the alert. But, if the worm is properly threaded on the hook, the fish cannot take it without hooking himself. As a rule he takes the bait with two tugs; the first is the process of getting set to crunch or to swallow the bait; the second tug is the completion of the operation. Ignore the first tug, but on the second, raise the rod tip with a swift, gentle lift and you will hook him.

Contrary to popular opinion, the Tautog does not have a soft mouth in the spring. Many fishermen believe that it has, and that, due to this condition, it will not take green crabs and fiddlers. The Tautog will take these baits at this time of year, but they are not too plentiful in the rockless, weedless bay areas where the Tautog spawns. Therefore the Tautog feeds on mussels and hard and soft shell clams, which are plentiful. He is not crab-minded, and particularly so since the soft food is all about him and is considered a delicacy by this fish.

Fishing along the shore for Tautog is best from the full moon in April until the new moon, or full moon, in July, providing the weather does not get too warm as the season progresses. When very warm weather sets in, the Tautog goes into deeper water and does not return until the last of August to then remain until the end of October. While the Tautog will take worms at any time during the day, the best fishing is to be had during the first two hours after daybreak and the last two hours preceding darkness. If the water, however, is very rough they cannot be caught because of their inability to see the bait. But should the fish, perchance see it, he strikes very hard.

Tautog swim along the shore amid rocks and weeds, and weed-rock beds, hunting for food, and there is always a hole where they will congregate. Should the angler be fortunate enough to find such a hole, he will have discovered a spot that will afford him excellent fishing for the balance of the season and, often, for seasons to come.

In both winter and summer the Tautog, a bottom feeding fish, is found in water of from fifty to one hundred and fifty feet deep. They will rise to chum in the bays, but since this is only an occasional occurrence it is not practical to chum.

I shall never forget my first party boat expedition after Tautog. It was back in my early fishing days and I went with Al, a friend of mine, and a veteran fisherman. We arrived at Sheepshead Bay just as our boat was about to cast off. The craft was crowded with fishermen mostly new at the sport, judging from their actions. Looking over the jammed boat, I could not figure how Al and I would have room on board from which to fish; every conceivable place was taken.

"Al," I said, "I think there is some mixup in reservations. That boat is full up. Hadn't we better postpone it?"

"Heck, no," he grinned. "Unless I miss my guess, half of those guys are out for the first time. Get aboard and I'll show you how to get plenty of room to fish."

We climbed aboard, the lines were cast off and the boat headed out from the dock. As we chugged along I noticed Al closely studying the anglers near him. We reached the fishing grounds, a forest of rods went into action, and so did Al. He took a stand close to three anglers who, nervously and uncertainly, were bracing themselves against the motion of the boat. Al coughed to attract their attention, and then apparently unaware of their presence, he produced a handfull of sea clams we had brought along as bait. Slowly, lovingly, he made a show of swallowing the clams. The three tried not to watch him but failed and soon Al's gastronomic display, plus the motion of the boat, had a drastic effect; ten minutes later we had ample room in which to fish. I do not, however, recommend this method as a means of procuring a place on a party boat.

Pointers to fishermen having difficulty catching Tautog:

When bottom fishing for this fish, take along a burlap bag containing either crushed mussels or clams, or a combination of the two. Anchor the bag in the water so that it lies on the bottom close to the spot where you are fishing and the Tautog, attracted by the smell of its contents, if present, will stay in the vicinity.

If Bergalls are stealing your bait as fast as you put it into the water, bait your hook with a whole live crab or with a soft shell clam, the shell left on. Bergalls cannot take this bait but the Tautog can, since he has the teeth and power with which to crush the shells.

Another way to foil the Bergalls is to use two hooks on the line; three if they are particularly active. Place the bottom hook about four inches above the sinker, the second hook far enough above the first so that they will not tangle in the water and; if using three hooks, place the third a similar distance above the second. Bergalls tend to cluster around one bait, so while they are ganging up on one hook, momentarily ignoring the other two, there is a chance of catching a Tautog on one or the other of them.

When fishing from a boat, you will improve your chances of catching a big one by using two hooks and putting two good-sized crabs on, one on each hook, for bait. Holding the claws folded against the body to prevent being nipped, place the crab face down and pass the hook through the right leg at the base of the shell and then push it on so that it will protrude from the left leg, at the base of the shell. Hooked in this manner, the crab will appear to be alive in the water even though it is dead.

Try fishing for Tautog with a 10 to 16 foot cane pole; 20 to 30 feet of 30 to 45 pound test line and use sea clams, steamer clams or small pieces of worms for bait. Just drop the bait in among some rocks and you'll have fun.

Tautog keep the head down and the tail up when taking bait so a long leader is not necessary.

Experiment by cutting bait in different ways and in hooking it in different ways. For instance, if using crabs, a successful method is to cut the crab in half, leaving all the claws on the half which is to be used, and then hook it through its base. Another method is to use the whole crab, hooking it through the back. With its claws waving about, due to the action of the water, it will, though dead, appear to be alive to the fish.

If fishing with worms and bites are coming few and far between, place a sinker of, say, 2 ounces on the line and, putting the rod in a sand spike, sit back and relax. Since Tautog cannot take a properly baited worm without hooking himself, your greatest concern will be that crabs may chew on your bait. So check it now and then and be certain that your reel is in free spool with the ratchet on. The ratchet will signal when the fish strikes and the Tautog hits so hard that, with the added weight of the sinker, the hook will penetrate into the jaw or, at times, even down into the stomach. When this occurs a disgorger will be necessary to remove the hook from the fish.

One day during the first week in October, a friend and I were fishing for Tautog at Narragansett, Rhode Island. We had an excellent location; rocky formations all along the shore, and had picked a spot where we believed we'd found a good hole. We were using small green crabs, whole, and, since the Tautog feeds as freely in the fall as he does in the spring, we anticipated a good catch. But, fish as we might, by mid-afternoon we'd caught only five fish with the largest weighing only seven pounds. Certainly it was nothing to write home about.

A lean, grizzled old timer in rather shoddy clothes came up, greeted us, and took a stand nearby. He was equipped with nothing but a hand line and a small can of bait. My friend and I, feeling a bit superior with our A1 tackle, wondered how the old fellow expected to catch Tautog with such an outfit.

As we watched, he baited his hook and made a cast close to where I was fishing. Thinking that his aim was poor because of using a hand line, I reeled in so as to prevent our lines tangling. But before I was able to retrieve my bait he had a strike. He had a nice fish on and, handling his line like an expert, he played it for a few minutes and then landed an eight-pounder.

I resumed my fishing and he continued to cast near me, catching four more Tautog right under my nose while I caught none. This convinced me of two things. First that we had a good hole, second, that the old fellow knew something about catching Tautog that I didn't. And I couldn't figure out what his secret was.

I must have shown my perplexity for he grinned and called over to me, asking if I would like to try some of the bait he was using. This offer stamped him as being a true sporting fisherman in my book.

I gladly accepted his offer and found that he was using a small bay crab that was new to me and had a shell hard as a rock. I put one on my hook and cast, and almost immediately had the rod nearly wrenched from my hand by a terrific strike. I played the fish and minutes later landed a fat ten-pounder.

The old fellow loaned me several more of his crabs and further fishing resulted in a nice catch of Tautog. I discovered in the process that the Tautog takes that particular bait with a force that is unbelievable for a fish of his size.

My new fishing acquaintance informed me that this crab is found in inland bays under rocks and weeds, and, since it does not live long after being caught, it must be used the same day. that it is procured. Which all goes to show that you can learn something from the other fellow regardless of appearances.

TUNA (BLUEFIN, GREAT HORSE	WEIGHT: Average 150
MACKEREL)	to 250 lbs.
Thunnus thynnus	Record—
Family: *Scrombridae*	1600 lbs.

There is no conclusive evidence as to just where the Bluefin Tuna goes in the winter nor as to where it spawns. It is found in waters that are practically worldwide, and off the Atlantic coast, from May until October, it ranges from Newfoundland to approximately Florida waters.

The largest member of the Mackerel family, the Bluefin Tuna is considered one of the fightingest of game fishes and anything can happen when a big one takes the hook. At the outset there

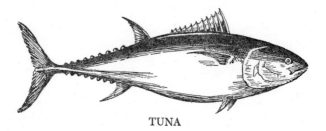

TUNA

is no stopping him and all the angler can do is to hold on, never allowing the fish a moments rest, hoping to break the Tuna's spirit before he, the fisherman, becomes tired out.

The Bluefin Tuna is a much stronger fighter than the Tarpon. When hooked, he may run amongst rocks and reefs, where a line may readily be severed, or he may take the fisherman for a forty mile ride out to sea. From eight to fourteen feet in length and known to attain a weight of sixteen hundred pounds, this fish is most abundant in the Atlantic, travelling in schools of from eight to forty or more fish. It feeds on crustaceans, plankton and smaller fish, herding the latter together. Bonitos and small dog sharks are also included in the diet. Shaped like a Mackerel, the Tuna's hide is so tough that iron harpoons are used rather than those made of wooden shafts.

While some large Tuna are caught in northern waters by trolling, the majority are taken from anchored boats, with a chum stream. Ground up Menhaden or Mackerel are considered the best chum.

The younger Bluefin Tuna, those weighing from 300 to 700 pounds, provide the best fight and it is the dream of every fisherman to land one of 500 pounds or over. Catching Tuna is not easily done, for, as a rule, many boats are congregated in a given area and large quantities of chum are thrown overboard. The Tuna feasts on the chum and is not readily attracted to the bait offered him. He has a disconcerting habit of closely inspecting the bait, and then, with a flip of his tail, leisurely swimming away.

I have often wondered if the bait offered does not, in some way, appear different and less appetizing than the chum. Or is it the way in which the bait sinks through the water? Would a cork, placed inside the bait, making it more buoyant and slower to sink, do the trick? Some day I am going to get around to experimenting with this idea.

Heavy tackle is needed for the Tuna. Use a 6 foot, 9 inch boat rod made of glass, beryllium or bamboo, with a tip weighing 36 ounces. A 800 to 1200 yard reel of 117 to 216 pound test line, 10/0 to 14/0 Sobey hooks and a stainless steel cable or wire leader 15 feet long. For bait: whole Mackerel, Whiting, Herring or Butterfish. High tide is the best fishing tide.

The Tuna either takes the bait gently or hits it hard, and once hooked, it is a battle of will-power and tackle against muscle—man against fish. Played up to the boat, apparently exhausted, the fish will suddenly call on some reserve power, surge away, and the battle commences all over again. But once the Tuna is boated it dies quickly.

Commercially, most Tuna are caught in pound nets and purse seines; a comparative few are harpooned.

TUNA (Small or "School")   WEIGHT: Average 40 to 100 lbs.

The term "School" Tuna is applied to the smaller edition of the Bluefin Tuna, fish that weigh up to one hundred and fifty pounds. In schools of varying sizes, this fish appears off the Atlantic coast during the summer months coming up from the Gulf stream to range as far north as Nova Scotia. They feed on plankton, crustaceans and smaller fish.

Trolling is the most popular method employed for catching the School Tuna. Use a medium boat rod with a 10 ounce tip, a 150 to 200 yard reel of 36 pound test line and 4/0 to 7/0 hooks. With this equipment the fisherman will have good sport and he will never forget the first Tuna he boats; it is indeed a thrill. Like their bigger brothers, the Bluefins, the School Tuna fight to the finish.

Once a school has been located and one of the party has a fish on his line, the fish should not be boated immediately. If played along in the wake of the boat, the other members of the school will follow closely, curious as to what is attracting one of its members. This action on their part affords the other anglers in the party an excellent opportunity to hook their Tuna.

Troll at nearly full speed and work the rod tip up and down through an arc of from two to five feet. Small feathers and spoons are good lures, and recently I've come to the conclusion that small plugs will also bring satisfactory results. Once the Tuna is boated, stand clear and let him flop about; he soon dies when out of water.

Tuna enjoy burrowing into the warm inshore sands and in disporting on the surface of the water, absorbing the heat of the sun, having a grand time for themselves.

WEAKFISH (SQUETEAGUE, SEA   WEIGHT: Average 3 to
TROUT)   12 lbs.
Cynoscion regalis   Record—17
Family: *Sciaenidae*   lbs. 8 oz.

A member of the Croakers, the Weakfish is often the first species of fish to be caught by the novice in surf fishing. An abundant fish, it migrates north in the spring and is fished for off the coasts of southern Massachusetts, Rhode Island, Connecticut, New York and New Jersey from May until October. It also ranges as far south as Florida and the Gulf. Spawning grounds are either far out to sea or in the large bays and sounds.

There are two varieties of Weakfish: the Squeteague or Gray Trout, which ranges north of the Virginia waters, and the Spotted Weakfish *(Cynoscion nebulosis)* called the Sea Trout, Trout or Speckled Trout, which is found off the Virginia capes and on south into the Gulf.

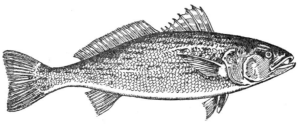

WEAKFISH

The only "weak" feature of this fish is its thin, brittle lips that are combined with rather tender jaws. Otherwise it is a hardy, well muscled fish and a sturdy fighter. In this respect a large Weakfish is comparable to the Striped Bass.

Time and skill are required to land the Weakfish, because, due to its fragile mouth, the hook can easily be ripped out. So it is advisable to include a landing net in the equipment, for if the angler tries to horse the fish into the boat, there is a good chance that the hook will tear loose and the Weak will be lost.

Weakfish will not die unless hooked through the eye, so do not hesitate to throw back any that are under-sized or that you have no need for. They will recover and live to be caught another day.

Fishermen always look forward to the arrival of the Weakfish in May, for it is the only species of game fish, with the exception of the Striped Bass, that can be caught in the early spring. And it is easier to catch than the Striped Bass.

Party boat fishing for Weakfish is very popular and the demand for boats far exceeds the number of craft available. So, if going on a party boat expedition, make your reservations several weeks in advance so as not to be disappointed.

One Tuesday, the second week in May, three of us headed for Peconic Bay and our first try of the season for Weaks. We had neglected to make our reservations in advance and when we arrived at our destination we found that there was no party boat available. Somewhat disgruntled we did the next best thing; we hired a rowboat and set out. After rowing for about three quarters of an hour we reached a spot where we felt we would have good fishing and cast anchor. We had light rods, 150 yard reels of 36 pound test line, 3/0 and 4/0 Sproat hooks and nylon leaders 3 feet in length. Our bait was sand worms and squid and we had live shrimp for chumming. While the Weakfish is essentially a bottom feeder it will rise to a chum stream.

We prepared our chum by pinching the shrimp between our fingers with sufficient force to stun them. If not stunned, they will be too lively and swim away and no chum stream will result when they are thrown overboard. We cast the stunned shrimp into the water; the chum stream formed and we let our lines out from thirty to fifty feet, live-line fishing with no sinker. The chum brought the Weakfish to the surface and when we quit for the day we had all the Weaks we could use.

Our next time out, having made our reservations well in advance, we had our party boat and some agreeable companions. Reaching the fishing grounds, we fished for about an hour having many bites but missing most of the strikes. Tiring of this, I decided to change my rig. I took a small piece of stiff wire and fastened it to the hook close to the upper end of the shank. I then pierced the head of a worm with this wire and put the tail on the barb so that the worm hung perfectly straight, its body free of the shank. This makeshift arrangement worked beautifully and, others copying my rig, caught a nice mess of Weakfish. The secret lay in rigging the worm so that it was in no way crumpled and the tail was close to the barb of the hook; each real strike meant a hooked fish. I made this experiment a number of years ago; today a hook is manufactured that permits the worm being hooked in this manner.

Should you, fishing from a boat with live-line and a chum stream, decide to go after only the big ones, add some weight, a pinch sinker or two of one and one-quarter ounces in weight, to your line. If there happen to be three men in the party, in order to ascertain the depth at which the fish are biting, one man can use a half-ounce sinker, the second man a three-quarter-ounce or full ounce sinker, the third man a one and a quarter or two ounce-sinker. One of these weights will probably determine the best fishing depth.

Boat fishing for Weakfish is done both day and night, mostly in small bays. If, during the daytime you should spot a big school of Shiners, Menhaden or other bait fish, you can rest assured that, come night, the Weakfish, if in the vicinity, will be after the school. The mouth of an inlet to a bay is always a good place, for the Weaks go into the bay at high tide, and again during the outgoing tide they swim back out through the inlet to the sea. Coves in the bays are also good fishing grounds.

August, September, and through the first two weeks of October furnish the best time in which to troll for Weakfish. Fasten a rather small bucktail fly to a spoon with a piece of pork rind or squid attached to the hook. Add a 1 to 3 ounce sinker, depending on the speed you are trolling. This additional weight should carry the lure down to ten or fifteen feet, the depth at which you are most likely to catch the Weaks.

When trolling, should you catch several fish in one area, the chances are you are over a school of them. Drop anchor and start casting, using the same tackle. Be careful to drop the anchor very gently so as not to frighten the fish below you, causing them to swim away. When you cast, let the lure sink down from six to fifteen feet before retrieving and then reel in slowly.

Daytime fishing should be done from a boat, trolling or chumming, because Weakfish do not feed on top to any appreciable extent during the day; they do not chase bait fish after it becomes light. If trolling for them, use small feathers for a lure and add enough weight so that the lure will sink down at least ten feet.

When bottom fishing for this fish, always fish with a slack line, and particularly so, if using worms for bait. With a slack line, the Weakfish will hook himself. When you feel that the fish is on, count 1-2-3 and then, very slowly, lift the rod tip. If fishing on a very calm day when they are usually sluggish feeders, count to 5 slowly before lifting the tip. If shrimp is used for bait the line can be kept a bit tighter than when using worms, because the shrimp, being a smaller bait, is swallowed more quickly than the worm. Excellent baits for bottom fishing are: Florida shrimp, bloodworms, sandworms, shadder crabs and squid.

If you fish with a star drag set, always remember to have it loose enough so that you can reel in quickly upon getting a strike. And when reeling in, keep the rod tip at the eleven o'clock position; the spring tension of the rod will prevent slack line after the fish is hooked and you start to retrieve. Permitting slack line, once the fish is on, is generally the cause of losing him. Do not, however, be too cautious; let him run if necessary, but pump the rod immediately if you feel slack coming into the line, for he has stopped running, possibly to rest, and you must commence reeling in again, immediately. But retrieve slowly.

Docks and breakwaters are good places from which to catch Weakfish. One day, about the middle of July, a party of us were fishing from a breakwater. As dusk settled upon us, scores of small fish suddenly began showering close in to shore, leaping from the water in an effort to elude something that was chasing them. We knew that their pursuers were Weakfish because the Weaks seldom splash water when in pursuit of bait fish and all the splashing was being done by the little fellows trying to escape.

Our fishing had been on the slow side, so, hurriedly we began to cast into the area where frantic bait fish were leaping. We made cast after cast, using every lure available, but had no success.

"What do you expect with all those bait fish there?" grumbled one of the boys. "The Weaks are there for sure but can't be bothered taking our lures."

"Aw, we're reelin' in too fast; we're too anxious," said another.

But I decided, after a dozen casts, that our trouble lay in the fact that while we were landing in the middle of the school, our lures were not sinking down to the depth necessary to attract the Weakfish. So I rummaged around in my tackle box and, tucked away in a corner, I found a lure I'd overlooked in my haste. It was a jig with a bucktail trailer attached 18 inches behind the jig. Quickly I rigged it on my line and cast, letting the lure sink down about fifteen feet. Nothing happened, due I think to the fact that I retrieved too fast. I cast again, let the lure sink down, retrieved slowly and a beauty took my bait. Nine more casts resulted in a catch of six good-sized Weaks. I passed the lure on to one of my companions, the problem being solved, the extra weight of the metal jig took the lure down to the proper depth to produce results. Taking turns, the rest of the boys, using my jig, caught a nice mess of Weaks.

As dusk gave way to darkness, the bait fish disappeared from along the shore and consequently, the Weakfish stopped biting. So we stopped casting inshore and returned to fishing off the breakwater. I decided to experiment with a bait rig, using a strip of squid on a regular Weakfish rig, such as is used along the beach. I baited the hook with a strip of squid, placing it just above a 2 ounce sinker on the end of my line. With this rig I cast again and again but did not get a strike. So I placed the hook six feet above the sinker and, since the length of the line made overhead casting impractical, I cast side-arm. Almost immediately I began catching fish; lengthening the distance between sinker and bait had done the trick; the squid, so rigged proved as effective as had the bucktail in the shallower water.

Generally, shore fishing for Weakfish is done from dusk on through the night, not in the daytime. But there are, however, in the spring and fall, exceptional days when they are migrating, and if the water is a bit rough, the fishing will be good.

Should you, some night, locate a school of Weakfish and you are equipped with a bait casting rod, a 3/0 or 4/0 bucktail can be used without a jig. Should you have a surf rod, a jig is necessary to enable you to cast out. Small plugs, streamers and small flies can be attached to the jig and often the smaller the fly, the better the results. Personally, I prefer a 1/0 bucktail, for, despite the presence of live bait in the water, the Weakfish will take this lure. Different feather lures are excellent for surf fishing for Weakfish.

Bear in mind, when catching Weakfish that they spoil rapidly. Always clean them the same day or night that they are caught, because if left around for an additional ten or twelve hours, they will spoil and will not be fit to eat.

Anytime you feel lazy and want to take it easy, put the rod in a sand spike, reel in free spool, ratchet on, and sit back and relax. The ratchet will signal when you have a strike.

SEA TROUT (WEAKFISH)

One winter vacation in Clearwater, Florida, I had great sport fishing for Weakfish, or Sea Trout, as they are called in those parts. The Sea Trout runs larger than its northern brother and it puts up an excellent battle. I fished for them from the shore, causeways and from boats, and, speaking of boats, they can be hired in the heart of the city.

I particularly enjoyed fishing from causeways, and often Edna, my wife, would accompany me, watching from the car and acting as my cheering section when I landed a particularly nice one. And then from the vantage point of a causeway, I frequently watched Porpoises chase bait fish close into shore. It was thrilling to see them leaping gracefully, glistening in the air, as they pursued their prey, a sight I appreciated even though the chase spoiled my fishing at that spot for the day. For with the arrival of the Porpoises, the Sea Trout stopped biting and became conspicuous by their absence.

The first day I abandoned my causeway fishing in favor of a boat I had to make the trip by myself. My fishing pal developed a migraine headache and couldn't make it.

Despite the fact that these waters were strange to me and I had expected him to act as guide, I decided to go it alone. I hired, for a very reasonable sum, a rowboat with an outboard motor and set out from a Clearwater dock. My tackle consisted of a bait casting rod, a 100 yard reel of 20 pound test line, nylon, and I had both artificial lures, and shrimp and squid for bait. I had also brought along my Sylvester float, my ace in the hole, on occasion.

It was a beautiful day as I cruised south down the channel. The white clouds overhead reflected in the clear water; the birds sang in the green boughs of the trees, adorned with Spanish moss, drooping down, in many instances, touching the water and seeming to nod to me as I passed. Combined with brilliant sunshine it brought peace to the soul and complete relaxation.

I knew that fish were probably under the hanging boughs, resting in the shade, but I was looking for a place where I knew they would congregate, a small cove with a sand bar. Riding on a rip tide, I was aware of the fact that the water would eddy into such a cove and that the Sea Trout would be waiting there for the bait-fish.

Some twenty minutes passed before I sighted such a spot. I cut the motor, drifted in, anchored and began to fish. I fished with live line with a float, using live shrimp for bait. A half-hour of fishing and I'd caught three Trout but they were all on the small side. The water was rather shallow, so deciding that I would not catch fish of any decent size here, I upped anchor and started out again looking for a similar cove where the water would be deeper.

A half-mile or so farther on I found my cove and the tide was making faster. Again I anchored and this time I used one of my artificial lures, casting into the place where the water eddied. I was rewarded with a catch of six Trout, the largest weighing nearly seven pounds. I should have been satisfied, I suppose, but I felt that by moving on I could do better. So again I set forth, keeping an eye on the right bank and, soon I found a third cove with a rather high sand bank. The water here was swifter and deeper and I decided to fish this spot out until slack high tide. By the time the tide had turned I had, using my Sylvester wood float, caught a dozen or more Sea Trout, three of them weighing over seven pounds. I was more than satisfied with the days fishing and very gratified with the performance of my Sylvester wood float. I had attached a small feather behind it and besides the Trout, had caught several good-sized Snook as well.

With the turn of the tide I could have reversed the process as I cruised back by watching the opposite bank for small coves. Here again, the tide now flowing north, the eddies would be formed in the coves and the Sea Trout would be waiting. But I had all the fish I wanted so I relaxed and chugged along, admiring the scenery as I headed for Clearwater. From every angle it had been a perfect day of fishing.

CHAPTER III

※

Striped Bass Fishing

STRIPED BASS (ROCKFISH)   WEIGHT: Average 5 to
Roccus caxatillis   40 lbs.
Family: *Serranidae*   Record—73
                                                              lbs.

Just the mention of Striped Bass quickens the pulse of every
surf fisherman who has ever experienced the thrill of landing
this fish. The Striped Bass, despite being tempermental and unpredictable, is much sought after by sport fishermen; it has
never fallen from grace with the experienced angler. It is a
true game fish and a fighter who, unlike some species of fish,

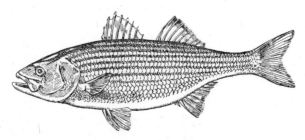

STRIPED BASS

cares nothing about rough water chasing bait-fish even at the
height of a storm. And it can stand both high and low tem-
peratures.

This fish is seldom caught in open water being generally
found near shore in salt, fresh or brackish water. It spawns in
fresh water where currents are swift.

Transplanted to the Pacific coast, along the Atlantic seaboard, the Striped Bass ranges from Nova Scotia to Florida being most plentiful from Massachusetts to the Carolinas. The waters off Narragansett and vicinity, state of Rhode Island, are undoubtedly the best locality in which to catch this fish. Here they are in great abundance. (Chambers of Commerce of other states may disregard this statement.) The reason Narragansett waters are unexcelled for Stripers is because they abound in rocky formations, sandy beaches, inlets, bars and breakwaters; every physical condition ideal for Striped Bass. To substantiate this statement, they are caught the year round. There is, however, a slight discrepancy that I must make note of.

For thirty years I have surf-fished, successfully, for Striped Bass in Narragansett waters. During six intermittent years of that period the months of July and August had to be written off as a total loss insofar as catching Stripers was concerned. Fish as I might, I caught nary a fish. Other anglers contended that the Bass had taken off for parts unknown, but despite my failure, I held that they had not, but were, on the contrary, not too far off. Subsequent study proved my contention to be correct; they had remained in the vicinity.

The reason for their disapearance was this. Wind and water conditions, consistently interferring for those two months with the feeding habits of the fish, they had left the surf of the shore and had slipped into nearby inlets and bays where the food was plentiful. Then as August waned, in each year, and with the coming of September a southwest wind set in, blowing steadily, the Stripers came out of the inlets and bays to be caught again in the surf both night and day.

When the striped bass is hooked, he takes off at high speed, running out the line and fighting every moment. True, there are occasions when he's caught without making a fight worthy of mention, but this generally occurs when he has been hooked in or through the eye; it seems to take the fight out of him.

Striped Bass are the largest close-to-shore-feeding fish. While they are essentially bottom feeders, they will feed on top but only if conditions are right i.e. when a southeast or northeast wind prevails. However, during their spring and fall migrations, when they are in big schools, they will surface feed even though conditions are not just to their liking. This is because in the spring and fall, bottom food is scarce and the Bass must, perforce, make the best of poor feeding conditions.

During the summer, conditions being right, Stripers will swim along the bottom gulping up crabs and the little sand fleas that are found along the water's edge. Just how a thirty-pound Striper can satisfy his hunger with these little fleas has always been a mystery to me.

The Bass do not attempt to feed when the water is calm and clear, because the bait-fish, able to see them some distance, can get a good head start and swim away before the Stripers can catch up with them.

I have come to the conclusion that the Striped Bass has a very poor appetite. When the water is warm, calm and clear they will eat a few crabs, sea clams and eels and swim offshore to find some rocks where they seemingly either doze or just loaf for a few days. Lacking the marked coloring of many species of fish, they blend into the background and it is likely that food, swimming unwittingly practically into their mouths, sustains them. If this be true there is no necessity for exertion; they can just loaf and enjoy life.

When they are in this state of inertia, you can row over them, see them and throw anything sinkable down at them and they will refuse to stir. About the only thing that will move them is a plug, which in the water acts like an injured fish; it'll arouse them to some extent.

Until comparatively recent years plugs were not used to any great extent in salt water fishing. This was because they were too expensive for the average angler. This is not entirely the fault of the manufacturer, for fishermen insisted on good-looking plugs, many believing that the colors attracted the fish. And, of course, this insistence increased the cost of manufacturing the article.

Plain plugs are less costly to manufacture and, in my opinion, they attract the fish as readily as the gaudy ones that are current in the bait and tackle shops. I don't believe color makes any difference to a fish and plain plugs would be much cheaper to manufacture.

To satisfy myself, I made several plain plugs, and the first opportunity to use them came shortly after I'd finished them, and with a grand guy as my companion. George Heinold, nationally-known writer and experienced fisherman, had written me that he was coming to Narragansett for some Striped Bass fishing. He arrived the day after I'd completed my job of manufacture and upon seeing the results, kidded me unmercifully. I just grinned and told him he might be in for a surprise. We got into Heinold's car and headed for a place I knew Stripers were generally around; it was not far from the town of Narragansett. Heinold was equipped with a light surf rod and some feather lures with which he had been quite successful. On his previous three trips he had averaged five good-sized Stripers and he was sold on the feathers as the lure to use.

We arrived at our fishing spot and he insisted that we fish with his pet lures. I put on one of the feathers but not too enthusiastically; the water was quite calm and I knew that this would make catching Stripers difficult. After an hour or so of casting, and we had not had a strike, I suggested that we switch to my plain plugs. "Okay, we'll give them a try," he agreed. "We certainly can't do any worse. But mind you, I'm doing this with reservations."

Several hours later we stopped fishing; Heinold had caught so many Stripers that his wrist was so tired he had to stop. The fish weighed from five to twenty pounds; a nice catch.

Driving home he happily admitted that my plain plugs were a success, "under existing conditions" but he still contended that his feathers were tops in his book.

"Just one of those days, Jerry," he grinned. "Tell you what, the next time we go out I'll take you on, you using your plain-Jane plug and I my feathers. We'll pick a time when the water is just right."

I'm looking forward to the contest, for I know that my plug will perform just as well under other conditions as it did in the clear water, probably better. The plugs I'd made act like a hurt mullet in the water, when properly handled, certainly an attraction to the Striper.

The Striped Bass is very tempermental and it is my observation that, year in and year out with all kinds of weather, the lure that catches them one day will not, necessarily, catch them the next time despite the fact that wind and water conditions appear to be identical. To offset the unpredictable feeding habits of the Striper, the fisherman must try to learn the habits of the fish; too many anglers tend to rely on some fancied lure and do not make a sincere effort to acquire a working knowledge of the Striper. Such knowledge is essential if one would qualify as a successful Striped Bass fisherman.

Mental laziness is the bugbear of most anglers. Time and again I've told my fishing companions of my findings only to discover later in the season when discussing Stripers that my advice had gone in one ear and out the other. They either hadn't troubled themselves to understand what I'd said, or they couldn't remember, or, worst of all, having caught a few Bass, they didn't feel that further knowledge in regards to the Striper was necessary.

Striped Bass are very difficult to catch, fishing bay-channels and inlets. They swim back and forth with the tide, so for the best results, the line must be cast across the current and, this accomplished, the lure retrieved so that the plug skips along the surface of the water, reeling in with long jerks on the line.

Again, the fisherman can walk along the shore until he sees a Striper break water, not too far out, and then cast his lure across the current, retrieving it so that it will come back again at approximately the place where he saw the fish jump. The chances are there is a hole at that spot where the fish has been lurking to dart forth to seize any unwary bait-fish passing by. So if the angler keeps casting at this spot the odds are in favor of the fish being caught.

Many inlets have bridges that span them and at times and during the outgoing tide, Stripers will gather to feed in the shadow under a bridge. During the month of October it is difficult to catch Stripers here because then so many bait-fish are coming out of the fresh water where they were born, swimming down with the tide, migrating to the ocean, and the bass, waiting for them in the shadow of the bridge, will touch only the food that comes down with the tide. Regardless of how attractive is the lure offered, unless it floats down with the bait fish, it will be ignored by the Striper.

A friend of mine, determined to catch a few Striped Bass from a bridge, had been unsuccessful. One day he came to me and asked if I'd go out with him so he could get a Striper or two. I agreed to go the following night when the moon would be full and with the probability of a northwest wind prevailing. I set the hour for our departure for one a.m., and he grumbled, wanting to know why so early an hour. I explained that the best time to fish for Stripers—and most other species of fish for that matter—was just before daybreak. It is at this time that the fish feed freely.

An October full moon shone from the sky as we set forth, and a brisk northwest wind was blowing, which was good. In October, this wind, prevailing during a new moon, or a full moon, will bring the bait fish down through the channels and inlets, hurrying out to sea. It still lacked fifteen minutes before daybreak when we reached our bridge. We had plugs and feathers for lures and my friend put a feather on his line while I decided to use a small plug. We made a number of casts, casting well up and letting the lure float down with the tide, but had only a couple of strikes which we missed. But as day began to break, the Stripers commenced to take our lures, and when, an hour or so later, we stopped fishing we had landed nine Stripers weighing from six pounds up to one fellow that tipped the scales at twenty-two pounds. My friend was highly satisfied.

However, the best way to fish an inlet is not from a bridge but to get a rowboat and anchor it in mid-channel about a hundred feet or so above a bridge. Drop your lure into the water and let the tide take it down under the bridge where the Stripers will be lurking. If there is no strike, reel in and repeat the process. Often the Bass will strike as you start to retrieve; your lure appears to be a bait-fish which has sighted the Striper and is struggling to get away, back up the current. Blood and sand worms, or a spinner can also be used as well as a plug or feathers on your line.

It is practically impossible to employ this floating technique from shore because the lure, though correctly cast, is generally carried quickly into the slack of the current and too near the shore for the Bass to chase it.

Ray Camp, sports editor of the *New York Times,* came to Narragansett one day for Striped Bass fishing. A sudden change in the wind had made the water extremely rough and Ray, not completely equipped, wondered if he could fish without getting wet. I assured him I'd take him to a location where he wouldn't get soaked. Reaching our fishing spot, I placed him on a fairly high rock then left him to go to another rock nearby. I hadn't gone thirty yards when I heard a yell. Turning, I saw the grandpappy of all waves breaking over Mr. Camp. How he kept his feet, I don't know, unless it was the strength of his language that supported him. Soaking wet, he fished; the ocean had played its joke; no more waves engulfed him.

Later, back at my tackle shop and fortified with anti-cold preventive, Ray told me in no uncertain terms what he thought of my prank. He was convinced I had planned it and I'm certain that only a fine catch of Stripers prevented the rupture of a beautiful friendship.

A word as to lures. I have found that a popping plug, one that rides on the surface and makes quite a commotion, is the best as a rule. A wood float with a spinner, baited with worms, attached behind it on a two foot leader is also excellent.

Should the fisherman prefer live eels to lures, place the eel on a leader that has three swivels, some 6 inches apart. These swivels prevent the eel winding his body around the line to resemble nothing so much as a backlash in the line. To appear natural and attract the Striper, the eel's body must hang straight in the water.

Surf fishing for Striped Bass has become increasingly popular with every passing year and it is necessary that the angler be properly outfitted. Wearing hip boots is not advisable because the waves will smack spray inside the boots, and, particularly in the spring and fall when the water is chilly, the fisherman will soon find that he is very uncomfortable. The outfit for surf fishing should be a good pair of rubber waders, a waterproof jacket with a belt that will tighten about the waist and hold both waders and jacket snugly, and any type of fishing hat the angler fancies. Waders with felt soles are recommended for fishing from slippery rocks, since the felt affords a better grip than does rubber.

Most of the best surf fishing lies near the outer rim of bars where the water is generally sloppy, and care must be taken not to be knocked down by the waves. Never turn your back to an incoming wave; never let one catch you head on in the stomach. Keep a constant eye on them and meet all waves of any size, sideways with the legs braced to prevent being swept off your feet.

Should a wave knock you down just remember that the water has a tendency to lift the feet and submerge the head, and this despite the fact that you have on heavy waders, for the upper part of the body is heavier than the legs. Above all, keep calm, paddle hard with your hands, paddling in circles, and you will soon be able to regain your feet.

Every fisherman wants to catch a contest-winning or record-breaking Striper and he should have the best equipment and know the best way of retrieving to enable him to handle the big one, should he ever tie into him. The chances are slim of hooking the big one, but should the fisherman do so, it would be a matter of lasting regret if the fish were lost due to inadequate tackle and poor technique.

I had this experience once and I'm positive that I lost the world's record Striper, a fish weighing from eighty to eighty-five pounds. How do I know since he got away? (I can hear the chorus, the big one always does). Well, I have fished for so many years that I have acquired the ability to judge the weight of a fish on my line to within a few pounds. For example: a fifteen pounder gives a bang-bang, jerk pull, a "pumping" fighter. A thirty pounder is far less bang-bang; less pumping with the rod is necessary to contain him. And from thirty pounds up, the pull is much steadier on the rod, for the fish takes off in a steady powerful run. Should you get a fifty pound fish, or over, on your line it will feel as though you had tied into a loaded cement truck going down hill.

In my years of fishing for Striped Bass I've caught quite a few that weighed from forty to fifty pounds and I've come to know the feel of a heavy fish on the line. So it was not too difficult for me to gage the weight of the one I lost. I repeat, in the eighty pound class.

I still wonder if I should have used a plug instead of the eel I was using at the time. A striper fights a plug and the lure is also resistant in the water and tends to tire the fish. An eel or a feather is easily swallowed, the plug rarely.

Plugs are also good as lures because they tend to keep the big fish near the surface of the water thus reducing the chances of the line being cut on any rocky ledges that lie farther down. Fighting the plug, and tiring quicker than with other lures, the fish is easier to land.

Remember, a plug with more than two hooks is not considered a good sportsman's lure; it is not recognized by the International Fishing Association. The accepted plug is one that has two hooks, set about six to seven inches apart.

Chumming for Stripers is done by many fishermen. To prepare the chum, use a meat grinder that is large enough to crush the scales and bones of the fish you decide to use. Either stale or fresh fish can be used and an ordinary pailfull should suffice. The chum should be thrown into the water, a handful at a time, at intervals sufficient to keep the chum stream intact. A pail full of chum should last several hours.

But anglers who chum the beaches are not too popular with other fishermen, and particularly so if menhaden is used, for this chum will travel along the shore for several miles and into all the fishing spots. Fishermen who have driven many

miles to fish this location and who, not aware that you are
chumming above them with menhaden and who are not using
menhaden for bait, will have their fishing spoiled. With menhaden plentiful, the Stripers will pay attention to no other bait
as long as the chum slick holds. And when the chum slick is
discovered, well, you supply the script.

There is one time, however, when chumming along the
beach is welcomed by all; that is during the month of August.
The chum attracts the Bass which, at this time of year, will
take artificial lures far more readily than they will the chum,
menhaden included. The chum brings them there and then they
take the lures.

MARCH

It was a pleasant, warm day in the first week of March
when three of us set out on a Striped Bass fishing expedition.
We had fished for and caught them through the ice during the
winter, using tilts, and now the time had come for our surf rods.

We drove to a bay which had a cove where the water was
brackish and fairly deep. This bay narrows down to about six
hundred feet at the cove, and about a hundred and fifty feet
from shore there is a bar with deep water on its south side.

Bars are always excellent places from which to determine
if fish are biting. If, however, the bar is located in a cove, the
fish will not bite unless bait-fish are around. So, if after a
reasonable time there are no strikes, it may be assumed that
bait-fish are not present and, no Bass. However, if the angler
has the patience to wait, the chances are that bait-fish will put
in an appearance, the Bass will follow them, and fishing will
be had.

We arrived as the tide was going out, the best time to fish
a bar, and began fishing in the deep water south of the bar.
We had surf rods, 200 yard reels of 36 pound test line, a three
way swivel attached about six inches above a 2 ounce sinker
and an 18 inch leader. We used blood worms for bait. One of
my companions used but one worm on his hook; the other, and
I, put on three.

We decided to fish the lazy man's way: we cast and then,
setting our rods in sand spikes, sat back smoking and talking.
Now and then a rod tip would dip but there was no signal
from the ratchet, merely a nibble and not a strike. This oc-
cured with increasing frequency and we finally concluded that

this early in the spring probably the only other fish which would be bothering our bait would be the Flatfish—Winter Flounder. So we reeled in, added a small number 10 hook to our lines very close to the sinker, moving our original hook two feet higher on the line. We baited the small hook with a worm and soon each of us had hooked a fair-sized Flatfish. We left the Flats on the hooks hoping that their commotion in the water would attract any Bass in the vicinity. Investigating Bass might take the original hook.

We fished the outgoing tide in this manner for nearly three hours before one of us caught a Striper, a ten pounder. Then they began to strike and during the ensuing hour and a half we caught six more, weighing from seven to fourteen pounds. But time had run out; the tide slackened and our fishing was over.

Coves in bays will harbor Striped Bass as late as July, but it is best to fish for them earlier in the season there because, as the water becomes warm, the Stripers start going out to sea. Start your fishing, in any instance, just before dark and contine on through the night.

Often crabs and perch will steal the bait. Try rigging an eel on the line, one about seven to ten inches in length. Hook it so that the barb penetrates about an inch from the base of the tail. This is important because hooking the eel any farther up towards the head will permit it to twine its body around the line, and not only will the Bass refuse a tangled eel, but it will be necessary to cut the line in order to remove the eel.

An eel, hooked by the tail, will swim about pulling on the line but not with sufficient force to set the ratchet clicking. Perch and crabs will not bother this bait, but when a Striper comes along, it being early spring and he is very hungry, he will not likely pass it up.

Should the angler decide to go after the larger Bass, a very effective lure is an eelskin and plug. The eelskin should be about two to three inches in width and from twelve to eighteen inches long. Slip the eelskin over any plug fancied, leaving about a half an inch dangling. This arrangement is readily cast.

If trolling with the eelskin and plug for a lure, troll deep enough so that the lure will bounce along the bottom.

Another good lure to use for Bass when trolling in coves is a spinner with blood or sand worms trailing from the hook. Troll along about a hundred feet offshore and keep the lure deep. If in a rowboat, the weight of the spinner is generally sufficient for the necessary depth. If using an outboard motor, however, it is frequently advisable to add a sinker of about one-half an ounce because the faster speed at which you will travel will bring the lure towards the surface of the water. But either rowing or using a motor, let the line out seventy-five to one hundred feet. Should you wish to slow the speed of the boat without stalling the motor and slacking the line, fasten a bucket to a line, and securing it at the stern of the boat, drop it overboard to trail behind the boat, it will form an effective drag.

One day, late in March, I was trolling with an attorney from New York in a large cove. We had hired a rowboat with an outboard motor and that motor proved to be the most temperamental one in existance. If either of us sneezed, it would either change pace or stall. We took turns trying to coax the darned thing into something like a respectable performance and finally the lawyer got it to running smoothly, but too fast.

Explaining that we needed a drag to slow down our speed, I fastened the end of a rope to a bucket and, passing it to my companion, instructed him to tie the rope to the stern and drop the bucket overboard.

A good man with a motor, he didn't know beans about knots. He tied the rope, dropped the bucket overboard and a moment later the slack rope was paying out and the bucket was dancing merrily away in our wake.

The lawyer made a frantic grab at the tail end of the rope, and followed the bucket into the water. As he went overboard, he managed to grab the stern and hang on, and, the motor conking out, we came to an abrupt stop.

I hastened to haul him aboard, spitting water and using words he never used in his bar examination. He sank down on a thwart, turned to me and grinned. "You asked me to provide a drag, Jerry. You can't say that I didn't cooperate, and then some. Br-r-r, this water is cold; can you get that darned motor started and take me to shore?"

Saying a prayer to the gods of all outboard motors, I turned to ours. It coughed a couple of times and then, a miracle, settled into a steady purring that was music to our ears. Running as smoothly as anyone could wish, it out-did itself getting us back to shore. We hurried to my car where I had a change of clothes, which the lawyer gratefully put on, and taking a little chill preventive, he came out of his experience with no ill effects.

We returned to the boat and, the motor running like a top, took it back to its owner. "I wonder why that danged motor had to wait until I got dunked before it would behave?" he asked, as we drove towards home. "You know, I think it's from a family of hot rods; it's allergic to trolling."

When trolling, and having live shrimp aboard, you decide to anchor and chum, pinch the shrimp between your fingers to stun them and then throw them overboard at regular intervals, a few at a time, just a sufficient number to form a chum stream. The stream formed, bait your hook with shrimp—or blood or sand worms if you have them—and let your line out a few feet at a time to about a hundred feet. Allow the tide to carry it out and keep moving the bait back and forth during the process. If the tide is running strongly use a 3 foot leader. Number 2/0 hooks are recommended.

If you fish with worms, from one to six can be put on a hook, but, as a rule, one worm properly hooked will prove to be effective. However, if several are used on a hook, a larger fish may be caught.

The phases of the moon definitely influence the feeding of Striped Bass. I have discovered that, granted the Stripers are present, the best time to catch them, in any month, is during the four days preceding the new moon. At this time the tides are swift and water conditions are exactly to the liking of the Bass. And year after year the Bass will return, at this time, to the same locality.

APRIL

In April—early spring—sea gulls cannot be counted on by the fisherman to determine if the Stripers are running. For, at this time of year, bait fish are so scarce that the gulls are not attracted. So during April, discount the gulls in favor of the calendar and start fishing about the time the new moon, or the full moon, is in the sky. You will find that the Bass are there, for rarely, year in and year out, have the moon phases failed to be dependable guides.

One bright April day several of us were fishing an inlet. We were using surf rods, 200 yard reels of 36 pound test line and artificial lures. We had decided on artificial lures despite the fact that bottom fishing at this time of year would probably be better. The water, though not rough, was choppy, and the tide was going out.

We cast our lures across the current and retrieved slowly, stopping our lures at intervals on top of the waves. We were trying to make the lure look as much like an exhausted bait-fish as possible.

For experimental purposes we used 3 ounce plugs and jigs, both large and small, but after fishing for an hour or so and getting no strikes, we changed over to very small bucktails and feathers and we soon began catching fish. When our fishing day ended we each had several good-sized Stripers to take home with us.

The following day we returned to the same place and now the water was very clear, so we decided that our best method to fish would be bottom fishing, using blood worms for bait. We cast across the tide and let it carry our lines until the worms were washed over to the bottom in slack water. The Stripers were there and we caught seven weighing from six to fifteen pounds.

If fishing an inlet that has a sand bar across the entrance, use a 4 to 6 ounce pyramid sinker. This should be heavy enough to hold the bait, generally speaking, in front of the bar, and fishing the outgoing tide chances are good for catching fish. When the tide turns and the rip is no longer there, reel in, go and have something to eat to kill time until the next tide. Or should you be feeling ambitious, you can catch them along the shore. If water conditions are to the liking of the Bass, they can be caught from shore on both incoming and out-going tides.

Casting from shore while fishing in the early spring, use lures that can be retrieved very slowly. A light block tin squid or, better yet, the wood float with feather, which is tops, is a good rule.

If the inlet has no bar, high tide is the best time for fishing with the first three hours of the outgoing tide a close second. There are occasions, nevertheless, when fishing will be good during the whole of the outgoing tide. This is during the four days before the new moon and for a few days during the full moon.

Lynne Lambrecht, sports editor of the *Providence Evening Bulletin,* had been after me for some time to go fishing with him saying he would take me to a place on the Cape where I'd

get tired of catching Stripers and, also, that he would outfish
me. I pooh-poohed the statement as a fish tale, mainly because
I didn't want to go so far afield from my tackle shop. Finally,
one day I agreed to go with him. He took me to the Cape Cod
canal where we fished all night and by morning, our catch
being nearly a hundred Stripers which we threw back. I'd had
my fill of catching them, besides, my wrist was so sore that
further fishing would not be a pleasure. As I propped my rod
against a rock, Lambrecht produced a scoop net and a hand
line and hook. He continued to fish with the hand line, landing
Stripers with his net until he'd reached the one hundred and
seven mark. He was using live squid for bait; they were in
abundance thereabouts.

Dawn broke and Lambrecht laid aside his tackle. "Well,
Jerry," he grinned, "I think I stopped you this time; I also
caught more Striped Bass."

"Yeah," I said, "but I didn't know you had a net, hand line
and free bait lined up. Certainly an ace in the hole, but next
time, old boy, watch out."

MAY

During the month of May the Striped Bass are migrating
and it is also the month when the bait-fish, crabs and worms
are plentiful along the ocean front, and the Bass feed continuously all through the day.

This is the month for the beginner, the would-be Striped
Bass fisherman, to go to the beaches as often as is possible.
Fishing conditions are most favorable and the novice has a far
better chance of successfully starting his career than in any
other month with the exception of October. In October, though,
the weather is generally chilly and the water cold, discourag-
ing conditions for the beginner.

The only poor fishing days in May are when the water is
calm and clear; the bait fish can then sight the Bass at some
distance and elude them; the Bass, therefore, do not whole-
heartedly attempt to feed.

Bottom fishing during this month is good, both day and
night. The sand and blood worms, migrating from the South,
number in the millions along the Atlantic coast and they are
a favorite food of the Striper. Squid, generally not a good bait
in the early spring, is excellent for the Bass during the last
part of May.

Should the fisherman elect to troll during May, he should use a deep-riding lure such as an eelskin or small feathers or an ordinary lure with a 2 to 4 ounce sinker added for additional weight. The lure should be small, the smaller the better, and troll very slowly.

A number of years ago, several of us were fishing for Stripers. We were using eels for bait and, although it was the middle of May, we were not at all successful. The swivel rig was not known at that time and the eels were tangling themselves up around our lines in such a manner that no self respecting Bass would give them a second look. The eel must be so hooked that the body will hang straight, otherwise it does not look natural and will not attract the fish.

We fished hard for several hours, staying with our eel rig, but not getting a strike, we finally gave up and went home, having no idea as to what was wrong with our bait.

Several days later I went out alone to the same spot. I'd given the matter some serious thought and believed I had the solution, a bottom rig I'd devised. It was a three foot length of wire to which I'd fastened swivels, spaced every six inches of its length. I strung an eel on this wire and it proved highly successful. The spaced swivels kept the eel's body from tangling about the line, and I caught several nice Bass.

One year, late in May, I went out from Watch Hill, Rhode Island, with Clark Gable, the famous movie actor. We found a place that was to our liking, a spot where we could cast into the right kind of white water. On his third cast, a Striper following Gable's lure, swimming hard, beached himself at the actor's feet. With a whoop, Gable seized the fish by the tail and swung it aloft.

"Look, Jerry," he cried, "he's undoubtedly one of my most ardent fans, throwing himself right at me."

Then the Striper, at least a twelve-pounder, wiggled loose and plopped back into the water.

"Humph," grunted Gable. "I hope my popularity with the fans lasts longer than it did with that one. Well, you never get anything worth while without working for it." He grinned. "You know, I love fishing whether I catch 'em or not. It's a hobby affording me complete relaxation. Without it I'm not sure I could take the strain of picture-making and do a good job of it."

JUNE

Along the East coast during the month of June, many fisher-men ease up on their Striped Bass fishing due to the fact that they believe it to be a month in which no large Stripers are caught. But I believe June to be an excellent month in which to catch Stripers, both large and small. June weather varies from spring to summer and the fisherman can adopt his fishing technique to that best suited for the weather-type of either season that he encounters when he goes out to fish.

It is true that not many large Striped Bass are caught dur-ing June, but this is due, I believe, to the fact that the wrong kind of lure is consistently used by fisherman. Until very re-cently the surface plug has been the almost universal choice; the under water plug has been passed by. In my experience, this plug is the one that will bring in the large Stripers during June.

The reason for my contention is this. The under water plug rides deep, where the Bass are feeding; the jointed plugs in particular when properly handled, will look exactly like a swim-ming herring to the Striper. He is very fond of herring and, lying in wait for them as they travel along the shore or swim out of inlets, he will feed on them all through the day and night. So during June try the under water plug, jointed pre-ferred, and you may be agreeably surprised.

While eels and eeltails are excellent bait, there have been many days when I'd better have stayed at home had I not had my herring-like under water plug with me. It brought results when everything else failed.

Should the angler, however, decide to use herring for bait, a fairly large one can be used—with or without a fish finder. Hook it through the lips or through the dorsal fin close to the body. Do not hook too deeply below the fin, for the herring will die. It must be used alive.

Baiting with herring, the reel should be in free spool and the line controlled by the thumb, exerting just enough pressure on the line to prevent a backlash. When the Bass strikes, the thumb should be lifted and the fish allowed to run with the line some seventy-five to one hundred feet. Then the pressure should be put on the line, setting the hook. This procedure permits the Bass to take the bait head on and then to swallow it. Should too much pressure be exerted before he accomplishes this, he will spit the bait from his mouth and will not return to it again even though it is alive and right under his nose. The Bass seems wary of a second try. Possibly this is because, through the pressure exerted on the line, the herring seems to him to have suddenly developed an unexpected strength that is unnatural.

During June the Stripers apparently lie up against the current waiting for it to bring the herring down to them. Evidently the current is so swift that the herring cannot turn back, once in range of its enemy, and it becomes an easy prey.

If fishing an inlet on an outgoing tide, using a lure, do not retrieve steadily across the current. Reel in so that the lure will drop back, then advance, then drop back again, for repeating this maneuver the lure will give a good imitation of a frightened herring that is struggling against the current, trying to escape.

A word on fishing with eels when herring are about. If a Striper hits an eel bait, he does so in earnest and with sufficient force to crumple the eel and knock it from the hook. Now, if the angler is getting hits without the hook being disengaged from the eel's body, he may rest assured that the Bass are just playing, bumping the eel with their noses and bodies. They are attracted to the eel but the interest is merely casual and playful; they are *feeding* on herring. In this instance it is best to change to the plug. It will simulate the herring on which the Bass are intent, and the fisherman may catch a few Stripers.

One night in June, Joe Chadelaine and I were fishing the entrance to a large bay. We were using surf rods, 200 yard reels of 36 pound test line and eels for bait. We knew that Stripers were present, hundreds of them, waiting for bait fish to come down out of the bay after the spring spawning.

On our way to the bay, Joe had argued in favor of using the eels for bait and I had finally assented to trying them. We fished for two hours but caught no fish. So I decided to discard my eel in favor of a deep-riding plug. With this lure on my line I shortly caught a beauty, a twenty-seven pounder, on my third cast.

Joe, still staying with his eel, laughed off my catch as an accident and refused to change his lure. But, after I'd landed two more Stripers of respectable size, he changed his mind and put on a deep-riding plug. When we stopped fishing we had nine Stripers, the smallest weighing twenty pounds, the largest —my last catch—forty-one pounds.

These heavy fish damaged our gear and lines and ruined our plugs. However, this did not concern us half so much as the fact that, due to using the wrong bait, we'd lost two hours of excellent fishing time, two hours of the high tide, the best time to catch them at this particular spot.

A week later I went out alone one night and, fishing with a jointed under water plug, caught three Stripers, the largest weighing forty-three pounds. Cleaning him, I found his stomach so full of herring that there couldn't have been room for more, and yet he had taken my lure. Often this is the case with Stripers; stuffed to repletion, they still will strike at that "last one passing by" and then, as a rule, spit it out. This rejected "last one" is probably the explanation why so many Striper strikes are missed; the Bass is full up, just fooling. But, in the case of the forty-three pounder, he fooled once too often.

The new moon never fails to bring the Bass and right on time; there is seldom more than a day or two variance in their schedule. The probabilities are that they are there all the time but are just not feeding. The coming of the moon seems to be the signal for them to make up for the hours of feeding they have lost, dawdling.

Should you be a new hand at the game, one who cannot tell by the condition of the water what lure the Stripers are likely to take at the time, you will have to experiment. Try everything you have with you in the way of lure or bait. And when you do land one, try to remember for future use what you had on the end of your line and what the conditions of the water were.

A pointer in regards to a prevailing southwest wind. Regardless of the type of lure you are using with this wind, you stand a good chance of catching a Striper. The southwest wind adds oxygen to the water and makes the Bass lively and more inclined to take your bait. But, in general, give each of your lures a fair try out. You will learn, and your knowledge will pay off eventually if not at the moment, and you may hit the jackpot.

JULY

This is a very pleasant month in which to fish regardless of the results. The fisherman gets away from the heat of the city to enjoy the cool ocean breezes and, if the fishing is slow, he can seek cover and enjoy an open air nap. And, relaxing or fishing, the salt air will induce a healthy appetite for the evening meal.

Fishing for Striped Bass in July can be very good or spotty and poor. At this time of year the Bass become very choosey as to what they eat. I believe that they have holes around sunken rocks or rocky ledges where they are content to lie in wait for bait fish to swim by, thus obtaining their food with the least effort.

If fishing along a rocky-bottom shore where rocks are jutting some few feet out of the water and the waves are washing over them, the lure must be cast so that the current brings it back between the rocks. Few fish will be caught when fishing such an area if cross tide retrieving is tried.

Should a Striper strike the lure and miss, he will not strike a second time; he will move away. But keep trying the same spot where he hit; a second Bass may have moved in and may take the lure. However, if, within a reasonable length of time there is no catch, it is best to move on to another rocky area.

One day late in July, I was fishing among rocks with Jim Hurley *New York Daily Mirror* sports editor. He was following my instructions, casting and letting the current bring his lure back between two large rocks that jutted some two feet above the surface of the water. On his fifth cast he had a strike, and missed it.

"Felt like a big one, Jerry," he said. He indicated several rocks clustered to his right. "Maybe he swam over there; it looks like a good spot. I think I'll try it."

"Better try the spot where you had the strike, again, Jim," I advised. "No telling where he went and, meanwhile, another Bass may have moved in."

He nodded assent and began casting in the original spot. On his third cast, a Striper took his lure as the current carried it back between the two rocks. Minutes later he'd landed a nice 8 pounder.

"Do you suppose any more will have moved in there?" he asked.

"You never can tell," I said. "Try again and we'll find out."

A dozen casts later and he had another strike that he missed and then, on his next cast, he again had a Striper, which he landed.

A most unusual occurrence, Jim Hurley then alternated between missed strikes and catches, all in the same spot, until he had caught six Stripers. Then the place became barren of results; cast after cast he made with never a strike. Finally he stopped, flexing his wrist.

"Six nice Striped Bass," he said, smiling broadly. "Unless my arithmetic is faulty, at least twelve Bass must have been lined up to play 'every-other-one-take-the-hook.' It certainly is a grand game."

"Good Lord! I never saw anything like it before," I stated, emphatically. "Evidently the bait fish were thick in that spot and the Bass were going to town on 'em."

Unfortunately the best fishing winds place the angler at a disadvantage because they tend to pull his lure across the tide current. But, if fishing from a pier, the cast can be made directly into the wind and then retrieved in the same direction that the tide is running and the current will bring in the lure. The lure will resemble a bait fish coming in from deep water.

Should the wind be coming from the east bringing short, choppy waves and clear water, Striped Bass are not likely to be found among sunken rocks and ledges unless there be white water. White water is caused by wind, tide and the phase of the moon and there is a saying among fishermen, "beautiful white water, no Bass will be caught." White water is beautiful for during, say, the first week of a new moon with fast tides, the waves breaking from one to two hundred feet from shore, create a foamy expanse of white water.

Now there are two kinds of white water and it took me many weary hours fishing to find out that one type is good fishing, the other poor. One condition is when, with a strong undertow, the white water is somewhat like champagne; all the fizzle on top and clear underneath. The waves are breaking but the white water is like a film over the surface of the water; it does not extend down to any extent. This type of white water makes for poor fishing.

While it is difficult to catch Stripers in champagne-like white water, they *can* be caught if the fisherman is not allergic to hard work. Using any surface plug or lure such as a spoon or feathers, he must cast out as far as he can and then retrieve as fast as possible, with quick, hard jerks so that the lure will roll and twist in the water. This technique is indeed exercise. It doesn't matter if the lure rides on top or under the surface;

the trick of catching the Bass lies in the difficult method of retrieving.

The right kind of white water is where the foam penetrates to a depth of two to three feet. Carrying oxygen with it, it exhilarates the fish and this makes for good fishing. In this kind of water the Bass will strike at the lure as it rides the crest of a wave, so the retrieve must be made in such a manner that the lure will act like a rubber ball, bobbing along on top of the waves.

A Striper will often follow a lure right into shore in this sort of water before he strikes. I've seen Bass leap clear out of the foam to drydock themselves on the beach. So always reel the lure right in to the white water at your feet.

If a strike is missed keep on casting, for in white water of the right kind the Bass does not go away. Keep the lure high-riding, the higher the better; the chances are excellent for a catch. Slow floating plugs are best, but a wood with a buck-tail behind is also good if allowed to float and retrieved only as it mounts the crest of a breaking wave.

If long waves are breaking about you, be on the alert so as not to be knocked from your feet. If standing in the water and a wave breaks behind you, do not, at this moment, decide to shift and lift your feet, changing your position. The backwash of the wave is powerful enough to sweep your feet from under you and flatten you into the undertow. This can be very dangerous. Stand still when a wave breaks around or back of you.

July 25, 1944. I shall never forget that date. It being war time, I obtained permission from the Coast Guard to fish from a certain high rocky formation on the nearby coast. Evening rapidly passed into a pitch black night, and, since I was not permitted the use of a light of any kind, I was fishing under difficulties.

I was equipped with a very light 8 ounce rod, a 100 yard reel of 18 pound test line and had a Japanese feather jig lure. On my first cast I tied into a big one that I judged to be well over forty pounds, but, being a bit anxious, I lost him. On my next cast I was positive I had hooked bottom, and then, the bottom began to move—and fast!

Now, ordinarily when a large fish is hooked, two or three pumps of the rod can be made before he decided that something is wrong and takes off. Then he will swim with a steady pull on the line until he either tires or is checked by the angler.

The big ones do not shake a line as do the smaller fish; they just try to leave the vicinity quickly and at a steady pace.

In this instance, I pumped the rod at least six times before there was any action; no wonder I thought I had bottom. But when the action did come, I knew that I had a whopping big fish on my line. Realizing this, I decided that I better move off the rocks to a firmer footing. The rocks were slippery, a condition which would add to the difficulty of landing a big one even with the aid of a gaff, had I had one with me.

Steadily playing the fish, I slid and scrambled down, and, on my knees at times, groped my way in the darkness to a small sandy cove I'd noted before darkness set in; it was about two hundred yards away. As I slowly progressed towards it, I continually pumped my rod, keeping as much tension on my line as I dared with my light tackle. Finally I reached the cove and better footing; now I could give my full attention to landing the whopper on the end of my line. After what seemed hours to me of fighting him with every trick I knew, I landed him. Actually it was just short of an hour from the time he took my lure until I had my fingers in his gills. He was a beauty! A fifty-seven pound Striped Bass, a world's record for surf fishing with light tackle and eighteen pound test line.

All through the fight, regardless of my position as I made my way to the cove, I was careful to keep my rod tip at the eleven o'clock position. Otherwise, the big Bass would have quickly broken my line and light rod.

Many fishermen, when they have a fish on, become excited or careless in the handling of their rods, and particularly so if the drag is on. Every second that they are playing the fish, the rod tip should approximate the eleven o'clock position; they forget this. Fewer big ones would be lost and fewer rods broken if the angler would but remember that the easiest way to have a line broken is to lower the rod tip, pointing it in the general direction of the fish at the other end of the line. I've seen many a line snap because the rod tip was held at seven or eight or nine o'clock instead of at eleven o'clock.

AUGUST

Unless fall weather sets in early, August is not a very good month for Striped Bass fishing. In August the phases of the moon seem to affect the feeding of the Bass more than in any other month with the possible exception of April. During the first week of the new moon the water is very active at times and fast rip, outgoing and incoming tides bring white water. But this white water is almost invariably of the champagne-type; fishing is poor.

With the arrival of the first quarter of the moon, the water becomes less active and the depth about static. This phase of the moon does not effect the rise and fall of the tides to any great extent and therefore normally good fishing holes must be abandoned for spots where the water is constantly deeper, for during this moon phase, the general lack of change in depth remains constant.

In the latter part of August, following the full moon, a condition arises which baffles me. The water is, for the most part, calm, the exact opposite of the water condition under this moon in other months, and it is full of phosphorous. So much so that, when fishing at night, a metal lure will shine brightly as it skims through the water. And at this time, the Bass become very playful. They flirt with any lure offered them but have no apparent desire to take it.

A tug will be felt on the line; the Bass will break water, and the angler will think he has a Striper hooked. He sets his hook, starts to reel in, then discovers there is no fish. Mr. Bass has just nudged the lure and then, with a leap, has swum away. He is just having fun.

I have experimented when the Bass are in this frame of mind by adding additional hooks to my line. I hoped that the fish, ignoring one hook, would take one of the others. The result was the same, no catch. The Striper would push and pull my baits and I've even found scales on one or more hooks, but the hooks were never taken. What has me talking to myself is the fact that the *feel* of a strike was there. How the fish can fool around in this manner and not be at least foulhooked is a mystery to me.

During the period of August doldrums you might, if you have the patience, try fishing with a float and bloodworms on a two foot leader. Cast out and let the lure float about, moving it gently once in awhile. You *may* catch a Bass, using this method, but any Striper I've ever caught, fishing in this manner, has not been worthy of mention.

Then again, you can try casting out and retrieving *very* slowly, so slow that the lure barely moves along the water. A friend of mine, Mike DeLucca, a most patient man, really enjoys this kind of fishing. He has, using this technique, caught more fish than I have during August, but none of a size or in quantity to cause me to imitate his method. Frankly, this technique bores me.

The latter part of August affords a perfect time in which to perfect one's casting. The water is calm and then there is always the offchance that the lure, cast in practice, may get a strike.

One day late in August, a summer resident of Narragansett came to my tackle shop. He wanted to go night fishing; would I take him out? I explained that during August the fishing was poor, often hardly worth the effort, but he persisted, saying he was tired of the nightly game of pinochle at his hotel and wanted a change.

We drove out that night to one of my favorite fishing spots, but we had hardly wet our lines before I thought that all the jet planes from Quonset were upon us.

It was a dark night with very little wind and there must have been a convention of South County mosquitoes in that vicinity. They descended on us in droves, attacking in formation. Fifteen minutes of slapping and cussing and we gave it up.

Driving back to Narragansett I was all apologies and mortified; I had forgotten to bring along mosquito lotion which would have greatly offset the marauders. I offered to go out again the following night but he didn't show too great an enthusiasm. As far as I know he resumed his nightly pinochle sessions for the balance of his vacation; I never saw him again.

SEPTEMBER

Four days before the new moon appears in the September sky is the time when the Striped Bass are commencing to form into schools for their migration, and, the weather cooperating, excellent Striped Bass fishing is in the offing. However, this is the month when northeast winds are likely to prevail and these winds bring poor fishing conditions along the beaches in certain localities. The wind stirs up the sand so that it hangs in suspension in the water along the shore rut or shelf, and the Bass will not feed. It is difficult for them to see the bait fish in the clouded water and the sand also gets into their gills.

When a northeast wind sets in, and does not change within twenty-four hours, it will generally blow for three or four days. When this occurs, give up any fishing plans for the fishing of a sandy bottom or beach; find a rocky bottom shore, a mussel bar or an inlet.

The northeast wind sets in as a rule during the time elapse between the arrival of the new moon and the appearance of the full moon. The water becomes very active. At this time mullet are migrating, and since they travel closer to the shore line than any other bait fish, the Stripers, pursuing them, can be caught in quite shallow water around bars and reefs. In my estimation, the mullet is a particularly palatable bait fish to the Striper.

The best way to determine if the mullet is running is to walk along the shore during the last three hours of the outgoing tide. If they are there, they can be seen bobbing and darting along as though pursued by larger fish. Mullet scare easily and when frightened will skip water at the slightest provocation. Once a school has been located, rest assured that the Stripers will be after them ere long.

When the mullet school arrives and you see Bass jumping, cast into the area where you judge the mullet are beginning to scatter in frantic flight. Make the cast and then let the lure float where it lands; do not start retrieving before you see Bass break water again. When this happens, reel in as fast as possible. The technique is to make the Striper think the lure is a lone frightened mullet which is trying to escape.

A mullet seldom wanders solo from the school so long as it is intact, so it is essential that your lure land in the school as it begins to break up, the members darting in every direction. The jumping of the Bass will signal the breakup to you.

The mullet skips along the water in his flight so the angler must, after casting, retrieve with short jerks so that the lure will act in the same manner as the skipping mullet.

Stripers will lie quietly near a ledge or along the beach when mullet are plentiful, not bothering to make a pass at the lure offered him; he is not interested in single fish. He is waiting for the school to appear and probably conserving his energy for the chase soon to ensue. When the school appears the pursuit lasts but a few swift seconds, the Bass darting after the mullet which are taking off in all directions. It is at this instant that the lure will appear to be a single mullet in flight. The school broken, the Bass return to their hiding place to await the appearance of the next school.

Two fishermen from New Jersey came into my shop one

day, the early part of September, seeking directions; they wanted a good spot for Stripers. I told them where to go; they bought a few odds and ends and some bait and turned to leave.

"Gentlemen," I said as they opened the door, "I think there will be a heavy fog before you finish your days fishing."

"Yeah?" answered the taller of the two. "That won't bother us; we fished in fogs off the Jersey coast and caught fish."

"That's not the point," I said. "I just wanted you to remember to mark the location of your car so you can find it when you finish fishing and start back."

"Think nothin' of it; we'll find it all right," said the one.

They left and within a couple of hours a dense, wet fog descended and I wondered if they had taken necessary precautions. They seemed to me to be a couple of the "we-know-it" boys.

Nearly eight hours after their departure they again came into my shop, two very disgruntled and tired out men. "Did you have a good fishing day?" I inquired. "How did the spot I recommended work out?"

"Fine," barked the tall man "It was good fishing and then that blankety-blank fog set in so thick you couldn't see anything thirty feet away."

"Yeah," said his companion. "We'd gone a mile or so down the beach, fishing, and when we started back we couldn't find our auto."

The tall man looked at his watch. "Hell," he exclaimed, "*eight* hours since we left here and we spent four of 'em looking for the car. Say, what d'you do in a case like that, anyhow?"

A practical method to insure finding a car parked back from a beach is to scuff a fairly deep furrow in the sand, pointing towards the place where the car has been left. The furrow can be as long as desired but it must be above the high water mark so that the waves of an incoming tide will not obliterate it. Walking back after having covered a mile or so of beach, interested in fishing, the tired angler, stumbling along in darkness or in fog, will encounter the furrow and then easily find his car. I know of one instance when a party of four, not having marked the location of their automobile, spent almost seven hours searching for it before they finally came across it.

I told my two visitors of this simple precaution and they looked at me bug-eyed.

"Well, I'll be a monkey's aunt," one exclaimed. "That's so blamed easy that it's no wonder most people wouldn't ever think of it. Okay, Mister, we'll remember next time."

A full moon in September, I've observed, will bring cool northwest winds and calm water. Under these conditions, the best place to fish for Striped Bass is in the deepest water you can find along the shore. While mullet can be used successfully for bottom fishing, I recommend using an eelskin or a weighted eel. Let this lure drag bottom as you reel in, retrieving with slow, short jerks.

On occasion, the northwest wind will give way to a wind from the east and the water will become clear and choppy. Many fishermen will persist in using eels then despite that under these conditions plugs are best. But should the angler stubbornly persevere with the eel, regardless, he should reel in slowly, lifting the rod tip as he retrieves so that the eel will ride the crest of the waves.

Deep-riding plugs when a northwest wind prevails, are good lures. Most fishermen fishing with plugs use too long a leader. The stainless steel cable or piano wire leader should not exceed 18 inches in length because when it is longer, the extra weight will drag the plug too deep. If the angler just must use a longer leader, the lip of the plug can be adjusted so that the plug will ride higher. This is done by forcing the metal lip down.

The only reason leaders of any type are used is to afford protection to the line against being damaged by the teeth of the fish or being frayed and/or severed by rocks. Some anglers believe that the color of the line or leader affects the fish in some instances repelling them and causing them to refuse to take the lure. I have no evidence that fish pay any attention to either leader or line and I don't think they are able to distinguish colors. This statement may cause an argument but I'll stick with my contention until I've conclusive proof to the contrary.

My favorite leader for Striped Bass fishing is an 18 inch stainless steel wire cable (on very rare occasions a 24 inch). This leader is flexible and can be depended upon not to break or chafe through on rocks or ledges. It is light enough so as not to interfere with the action of the plug in the water.

Should you intend to fish among rocks or over a rock ledge with a nylon line and have no steel cable leader at hand, add to the nylon about 20 feet of linen line. This extension will guard against fraying on the rocks, as the linen will not chafe as readily as will nylon.

The length of a nylon leader doesn't matter, since nylon has no effect on the action of the lure. But nylon lines have a tendency to weaken after several hours of casting, so feel them every so often to make sure that there are no frayed spots. And when testing your line, examine the guides to be certain that there are no small nicks or grooves which will shred the line as it passes through.

I was fishing one day with David Niven, the movie star. We were on a rocky shore, the rocks were very slippery and the going was rough. Both of us were sliding and skidding and Niven had narrowly escaped going into the water on several occasions. Finally he called to me.

"I say, Jerry, isn't there some way in which Striped Bass could be induced to frequent only nice, sandy beaches? To make a go of it on these rocks, a chap has to emulate a ballet-trained goat which has six legs, a rudder for a tail and a charming disposition. And I never fancied being a goat."

Moments later he had a strike, and skillfully handling his rod, he landed a twenty pound Striper. Shortly after he had another, this one weighing twenty-six pounds.

Niven grinned, delightedly. "You know, if this is the reward, I shall gladly become *any* goat, human, mountain or otherwise if by so doing I can continue to catch 'em like this. That is, temporarily, you understand, Jerry."

Providing weather conditions are right, all the bait fish that the Stripers like will be around during September. Watch the action of the sea gulls; if they are feeding or sitting on the waves in a certain area it will indicate that the bait fish are there. The gulls are waiting for the Bass to come and start feeding on them. Along shore, if you should see gulls staying near the entrance to a cove, keep your eye on this spot. If the birds are attracted by bait fish there, the Stripers will put in their appearance. They may arrive as you are watching or it may not be until the change of the tide. So be patient.

While you may catch Bass at half tide it does not necessarily mean that you will catch them at the same place at high tide; Bass like to feed at a depth that is almost constant.

September is a fine month for catching the larger Stripers. I know the thrill of landing the big ones and how difficult it is not to get excited, particularly if it is the first big Striper. I realize how difficult it is to remain calm, but the best known way to lose a big fish is to get excited and hurry the process of trying to land him. While realizing that he is contending with a very worthy antagonist, the fisherman *must* relax if he is to come out the winner.

I have experimented with this problem of relaxation. All living creatures will fight that which deprives them of their freedom, and fish are no exception. I do not believe that fish feel pain, but when hooked and they feel the pressure on the line forcing them to go in a certain direction, instinctively they will fight against this force.

One day, this theory in mind, I hooked a large Bass and then let him run the line out about two hundred yards. I then put enough pressure on the line to stop him and, once stopped, I laid the rod down on the sand and waited for the fish's next move. The pressure removed, he made no effort to swim farther away, but the moment I picked up my rod and began to reel in, the fight was on. The Bass had no desire to go in the direction in which my retrieving was forcing him. I've made this experiment with different species of fish and the result has been invariably the same in every instance. If the fish is firmly hooked and the angler knows how to handle his rod and reel, he can set his time, as a rule, for landing him. If not firmly hooked, the hook will soon rip from the mouth of the fish and he will be lost.

I generally use light tackle: an 8 ounce rod, 200 yard reel and 20 pound test line of linen or nylon. I have found that fishing with free spool the fish can be turned with light pressure, using my thumb on the line as a brake.

One day I was fishing with Ray Trullinger, fishing editor of the *New York World Telegram,* and I hooked a thirty-five pound Striped Bass. I was using my favorite lure at that time, a dark lead feather jig. The fish took off quickly and swam under a rocky ledge from which I could not budge him.

"Well, maestro, what do you do now?" asked Ray. "You can't horse him out with your light tackle and it looks as though he'd taken up residence for the season."

"Just relax, Ray," I said. "I'll show you a little trick."

Permitting plenty of slack line, I snuggled the rod under my arm and sat back, confident that my linen line would not chafe readily against the rocks.

Ray stopped fishing to watch proceedings; we lighted up and sat back and chatted. While talking, I constantly tapped the rod with my hand.

"Why the gentle tapping, Jerry?" Ray finally asked. "You nervous?"

"Nope! I'm trying to annoy Mr. Bass so that he will decide to leave where he is for some place where he won't be bothered."

Six cigarettes later, the fish, finding no pressure on the line, and I believe annoyed by the tapping, left his hiding place, and I landed him. Had I tried to force the issue, my line would probably have been severed by the rocks and I would have lost a nice fish.

If fishing from high rocks or from a high ledge, always have a place nearby to which you can go once you have hooked your fish; a place that is low enough so that you can get the fish by his gills to lift him from the water. Start making your way to this spot while the fish is on the line and he is still quite some distance out. Play the line constantly as you walk along. Having arrived at your "landing area," you will find it easy to bring him in at about the exact place where you wish to land him. This cannot be done from a high rock or ledge. I have landed many Stripers when fishing from a breakwater by following this procedure. A gaff can be employed, but preferring the method I've just described, I never carry one. Once the fish is exhausted and within reach, it is easy to lift him from the water by his gills.

Always remember that a landed fish, thrashing about, can be very dangerous due to the hooks on the plug that is still in his mouth. A twelve pound fish will thrash more violently than a forty-pounder so, there is, therefore, more danger of being snagged by the hooks in the mouth of the smaller fish than by those in the larger. Protruding from the fish's mouth, the hook, or hooks, on a plug can inflict a nasty wound in the hand, leg or face of the careless angler.

The best way in which to avoid this hazard is to always be provided with a mallet. The moment the fish is landed, knock him into submission with it. Should you not have a mallet, the next best method is to step on the fish, and holding him down, get your fingers firmly in his gills and then extract the plug. If you are not confident that you can accomplish this successfully, then leave the plug in his mouth and continue fishing with another plug. The fish will thrash around until he is exhausted and then the plug can be safely removed.

One night I went against the advice I've just given—and to my sorrow. I had hooked a fourteen pound Striper and, rushing him in, I landed a fish that was still full of fight. It thrashed about all over the place. I stepped on him, not as firmly as I should have, reached for his gills, my foot slipped and bam! One of the hooks of the plug sank deep into the base of my thumb. The fish threw himself about with great violence and, willy-nilly, I had to follow his gyrations until he exhausted himself. To a casual onlooker, the situation would probably have appeared humorous, but to me, painfully hooked to a flopping fish in the dead of night, it was far from being a laughable situation.

Should you hook a Striper that takes off with a steady pull, you have one on the line that is either a big one or one that has been foul-hooked. Let him run with the line, the drag loose, until, feeling he has taken line enough, start turning the drag to the right, a little at a time, in order to check him. Do not tighten the drag too abruptly; the biggest fish are often lost near shore because of doing this. The Bass may seem to be exhausted, but almost invariably he gives a last surging fight for freedom, and, if the drag is too tight, something must give. Generally it is the line, not the jaw of the fish.

October

This month offers both poor and good fishing, depending upon weather conditions. Generally towards the end of the month, the weather becomes uncomfortably cool; the water temperature drops, becoming cold, and the bait-fish are affected. The cold water slows them down and they experience difficulty when swimming against a tide, and thus become easy prey to the Striped Bass as they drop back, exhausted. With food easy to get and plentiful, the Stripers feed freely and this makes for good fishing.

If, during October, a windy period sets in, the bait-fish will swim close in along the shoreline and the Bass feed on them day and night. Early morning or just before dusk, fishing from a boat, is the best time to go after them. However, if you want midday fishing, sit on the shore and wait until the Bass come even closer—they frequently do—and the chances are, your patience will be rewarded.

During October, the sea gulls are especially helpful in locating the schools of Striped Bass, this during the day time. At night the angler must depend on his knowledge of the tides and the feeding habits of the Striper, a creature of habit.

One very calm day I watched sea gulls follow a school of Striped Bass in quite close to shore. The school remained for a few minutes and then swam out again to an area some five hundred feet offshore and on the edge of a rip tide. Here they stayed, waiting for bait-fish to put in an appearance. The gulls, hovering over them, betrayed the presence of the school all the way.

If a boat had been available, it would have been the time to go after them. For, remaining in that area and a good number of Bass breaking water, I knew that for every Striper I saw leap from the water there were hundreds more beneath him in the water—a grand fishing opportunity.

Fishing one day from shore into rough water, I could see the smaller fish in a school of Striped Bass swimming about directly in front of me. Out beyond them, about where the third and fourth row of waves was breaking, I knew the large members of the school were located. Casting in front of this school had brought no catch, so I commenced to cast beyond the school, retrieving slowly through it, and the Bass began to strike. I caught several nice Stripers.

But I grew tired of seeing the larger ones breaking only some three hundred or so feet out. I suggested to a friend who was with me that we get a boat and go after them. We procured a skiff, rowed out, and, anchoring near the school, began casting right into them. The Bass began breaking all around the boat, a thrilling sight, but they refused to take our lures.

After some thought, I decided that we were using the wrong technique. So we changed, letting our lures sink down about twenty feet and then retrieved slowly, with a drop back, then bringing our lures to the surface. This method worked beautifully; we caught several six to twelve pounders and four that weighed from twenty to thirty-two pounds.

If, on occasion, you locate a school of Bass but cannot at the moment fish for them, place the location of the school in your mind by any available landmarks, and allowing for the time difference of the tide, return an hour later the next day to the same place. During the interim the school may have moved a mile or two in one direction or another, but it will be in the

general vicinity and the sea gulls will indicate the new location
to you. Striped Bass habitually feed best on the incoming and
outgoing tide; at high tide they seem to stop for a rest.

One night a fisherman came to me, wanting me to go out
with him for Stripers at a spot quite some distance away. He
had read that several large Bass had been caught at this place—
no other locality would do. It took all my powers of persuasion
to convince him that when the Striped Bass are hitting, actively
feeding at one place, almost invariably they will be biting all
along the immediate coast line.

He finally agreed with great reluctance to accompany me to
a spot I knew some five miles closer than the place he had in
mind. Here we fished and he caught four ten to eighteen
pound Stripers.

"I guess you knew what you were talking about, Jerry," he
said as we shook hands good night. "This experience will stop
my rushing off to every spot that I read of where Stripers are
reported caught. I'll try closer home next time."

When the weather is cold, the big Stripers can be caught at
any time of day, even in calm surf. However, as the season
progresses and becomes colder, I recommend bottom fishing.
Build a good fire on the beach and set your rod in a sand spike,
using live eel or whole fresh squid for bait. When using squid,
use a tandem hook, size 6/0 to 8/0 in size. The head of the
squid should be near the top of the shank; the tail on the barb
so that the squid will hang straight and not crumble in the water.

If the angler decides to go out only for the Big One he must
be prepared to exercise patience; the big Striper does not strike
as readily as his smaller brethern and, during migration, the
feeding time is of short duration. To hook and land one requires
hard and consistent fishing for days and nights and even for
weeks. The best fishing time is during the period of the new
moon when the big Bass feed best, with the full moon a good
second choice. The angler never knows on which tide they will
feed, sometimes low tide, again, high tide. Therefore the fisherman must fish the tides in and out. In my experience, as stated
before, the eelskin over a plug is probably the best lure for the
big Striper.

One day late in October, Larry Tessier joined me to go out
for a try for a big Striped Bass. We drove to a location where
we could fish from a rocky formation. After a little while I
noticed that Larry was having difficulty keeping his balance
on the slippery rocks.

"Hey, Larry," I called, "you look like you'd had, not a couple, but a half dozen stiff ones."

"Wish I had, Jerry," he said, "It's darned cold and these rocks are as slip—Yowie!"

His feet went out from under him and he took a header in between two large rocks.

Dropping my rod, I hurried over to rescue him, nearly taking a ducking myself as I scrambled along. I helped him out of the water and we scurried back to the car where there was a change of clothing which Larry had had the foresight to bring along, always a sensible precaution.

"Don't you know, fella, that the chances of catching a big Striper by diving in after him are about one in ten million?" I kidded.

"Aw, shut up, and go to," he grunted, as shivering, he changed into his other clothes. "I suppose the great Sylvester never took a header."

"Yes, I have, but not often," I replied. "You know, Larry, if when you recently bought those new waders you had taken my advice and purchased a pair with felt soles, the chances are you wouldn't have slipped and fallen into the water."

"Okay. Right as usual," he chattered. "Let's get going; I've got the shakes. I think it's a plot, but come on, we'll go back to that tackle shop of yours and I'll buy a pair of felt-soled waders."

NOVEMBER

Fishing for Striped Bass during November is a cold sport, but once the migrating schools are located, the fishing is good. The Bass can be caught both day and night because, being on the move, they feed freely and will take the lures offered them.

The inlets and bays are excellent localities in which to fish. The Bass follow the tide in and then, if bait-fish are not plentiful, at the turn of the tide they follow it out again to sea and then repeat the performance. Ordinarily, going in they seldom progress farther than about a mile into the bay. This routine continues until real winter weather sets in.

With cold weather the Stripers which are remaining in the bay seek the deepest water they can find and remain there, deep down, until the weather breaks and a warmer season sets in.

Generally speaking, large plugs are not effective in inland waters but there are days when the Bass will take any lure that is on the line. Small plugs, streamers and small feathers are best for both casting and trolling. Sand worms and blood worms are also excellent for trolling.

During November, a rowboat is better than shore fishing. The exercise or rowing helps one to keep warm and permits the angler to cruise around in search of a cove or bar where the Bass are feeding. This can be determined by simply catching one or two or by seeing the fish break water.

Off the coast of North Carolina, the water remains open all winter and the angler can take advantage of this fact. He does not have to turn to ice fishing as he does farther north.

December Through February

I cannot speak for winter conditions in Chesapeake Bay because I am not familiar with them. But fishing farther north, during the months of December through February is to me far from a joyful sport. However, if there should be a bay in the vicinity where Bass are wintering, and there is no ice, dress warmly, apply vasoline to hands and feet, be sure the ears are covered and use a rowboat to either troll or cast. It is possible that your catch will reward you for your hardihood, for if you don't catch Stripers you will probably get White Perch, a fish that is delicious to eat in the winter time.

December, January and February are cold months, but sometimes the ice is late in forming or an unseasonable thaw will cause open water. I follow a certain method for discovering if the Bass are there on a cold day with open water. I park my car along the frozen beach, and lowering the window a couple of inches, sit and listen for the sound of the fish breaking. If after a reasonable length of time I do not hear them, I drive on a bit and repeat the procedure. It is far better than walking along the beach and I prefer to know that the Bass are there before wetting my line.

Fishing is fun and a Striped Bass dinner is as tasty in December as any other month, but when the weather becomes too cold for comfort and the angler has to grease hands and feet for protection against the cold, I'll settle for some other meal from the sea—little neck clams for instance. Digging the clams, I keep warm and still can anticipate a sea food dinner.

Little neck clams are dug up from around rocks, and since sea food is all pretty much the same to me, I am pretty well satisfied with a dozen or two. My great interest is in catching fish, not in eating them. I do not recommend ice-fishing during the cold months because it can be a dangerous sport. The rise and fall of the tides can cause the ice to break up quickly and without warning unless it is quite thick. The angler should not attempt it unless there is a freeze of from three to four inches, preferably more.

I respect the potential danger of heavy waves and of ice. I am a sissy in regards to the latter; I will not set my tilt unless the ice is six or more inches thick. Even this ice can be broken up in no time by a heavy, fast-rising tide and with little warning.

Many fishermen maintain that Striped Bass hibernate throughout the winter months and, therefore, will not bite. Possibly they do hibernate, but fishing through the ice I have found that Stripers will take bait. They have been caught all through the winter from rivers and bays all along the Atlantic coast.

If you decide to go ice fishing, take a hand axe and cut a hole in the ice about twelve to eighteen inches across. Use shiners, mummies, small eels or worms for bait. Set your tilts, one to each hole you cut. The tilts can be left over night if either you have no shelter or if you do not care to remain at the holes all night. Many dyed-in-the-wool ice fishermen have shelters made of plywood or plywood and canvas, some four to five feet high. Set up on the ice near the hole, shelter is provided on three sides. Kerosene heaters placed on a wood plank afford heat.

Fish with a line of from 20 to 36 pound test with a leader 18 inches long. The line is, of course, fastened to the spool on the tilt. Find bottom and then slip-loop a 2/0 to 4/0 hook on the line so that when baited, it will hang about three feet above bottom. The reason for slip-looping the line is this. When the Bass takes the bait, the loop will slip loose and the line will pay out. He will thus have enough line—three feet— so that he can lie on the bottom until signalled by the red flag on the tilt. The angler can come and land his fish. Without the extra three feet, the fish would be suspended that distance above the bottom, and swimming around in his effort to free himself, he will chafe the line on the edge of the hole until it finally parts.

Should the angler not care for the slip-loop arrangement, he can use a steel cable as a line; this will resist the chafing on the ice.

Most bays along the coast will shelter Striped Bass during

the winter months. I believe that the schools of Bass that migrate to our northern shores would remain here permanently if there was enough water to accommodate them. I have for years noted that the schools of smaller bass will arrive and stay in these waters for several years, remaining until they reach the average weight of about 25 pounds. Then these schools that I've had under my observation will disappear and their place will be taken by other schools similar in size and weight of the departed schools when they first arrived. And through the years this performance has been repeated at regular intervals. Arriving at an average of about 25 pounds seems to be the signal for the resident school to depart and a smaller school to arrive and take its place.

So, if the spawning grounds here were large enough, I believe that the schools would continue to arrive and not leave the general vicinity. They would stay here permanently to afford wonderful Striped Bass fishing.

CHAPTER IV

Tackle, Place and Season

Spinning

FOR A NUMBER OF YEARS I have been an advocate of the use of light tackle for salt water fishing; it does not tire the fisherman as readily as does heavy tackle and it gives the fish more of a sporting chance. Now Spinning is coming to the fore.

Spinning tackle is essentially that of the fresh water fisherman adapted to salt water fishing, but the reel is of an entirely different construction than that of the standard reel. Unlike the standard reel, the spool does not revolve. The line, impelled by the force of the cast, spills off the end of the reel and is wound back on to the spool by a pick-up arm that revolves in but one direction. Due to the construction of the reel a backlash is practically impossible, and thus, the main hazard in learning to cast is removed.

Spinning rods are from seven and a half to ten feet in length and made of glass or bamboo. They weigh from five to sixteen ounces and have a "whip" to them. The Spinning lines, made of braided nylon or monofilament, are from six to twenty-six pound test; the lures used weigh from one-half to three and a half ounces. The guides, together with the reel, are aligned on the under side of the rod, the reel being attached to the butt some ten to twenty-four inches from its end.

The butt of the rod is held with the thumb on top and the hand underneath with two fingers in front of the reel support, two fingers behind it.

In learning the art of Spinning, cast gently, then as you become familiar with the feel of the rod and action of the reel, slowly increase the power of the cast. The line should be released by lifting the index finger from it when the rod tip approximates the eleven o'clock position.

The tendency of most fishermen new to Spinning is to steady the line with the *joint* of the fore finger. The proper manner is to use just the tip of the finger; it is easier to let the line spill off the reel with the snap of the rod. Also, using just the tip, the hazard is removed of having the finger joint cut or burned as the line pays off.

When retrieving, do not permit the reel to back up. Backing up is caused when a lapse is permitted during the process of reeling in and the line will then loop into what approximates a backlash.

It is a big temptation, particularly for the beginner, to use force when casting in the expectancy of seeing the lure sail far out. If the angler will go about casting gently it will pay off in the long run; he will learn the necessary and desired control of the rod and reel without forming bad habits which will have to be overcome. He must remember to cast with a hand and wrist action; *not* with the arm or shoulder.

A gaff hook is handy to have if a big fish is hooked. It is not, however, absolutely essential if the fisherman will keep calm and let the waves assist him in landing the fish. Nearly all well-hooked fish get away when, apparently exhausted and brought close enough to gaff, they call on that last reserve of energy and make a surge for freedom. When this last effort is made, and the fisherman has no gaff, he should allow the fish to drop back, wait until the next wave lifts him towards shore and then gently exert pressure on the line. A particularly stubborn fish may make it necessary to repeat this procedure several times before he is landed.

When spinning, the angler becomes a real sport, for using light tackle, easily broken if not properly handled, he affords the fish a far greater chance to defeat his efforts to land him than he does when he uses heavy tackle. A fish of any decent size cannot be horsed in with spinning tackle. True, fishing in this manner, the quantity of fish caught will suffer, but as much satisfaction, if not more, will be derived from landing one or two large fish than if a dozen had been caught with heavy tackle.

Considered at first a novelty, many fishermen are taking up spinning in a most serious manner. I believe that more women will become anglers through spinning; it is easier to learn and makes for easier fishing than does the standard reel and rod.

One night a number of anglers were fishing off a jetty for Striped Bass. A man and woman stood near me, evidently husband and wife. They were equipped with spinning tackle. Shortly after I'd noticed this fact, she tied into a big one and those of us near her stopped fishing while she played him. This was not out of politeness due to her sex, but because it is the sporting thing to do so as not to entangle the line of the angler who has hooked a fish.

She played the Striper for an hour before landing him; a forty-five pounder. During her fight with the fish, I heard a grumble or two from nearby fishermen in regards to the time being lost. True, other Stripers may have been caught during that hour, and probably big ones, because only the large ones seemed to be in this vicinity, but by being good sports, albeit somewhat unwillingly, the other anglers were unconsciously conserving Striped Bass. For it is the large Stripers who produce the most eggs every spawning season. Somehow I'm afraid that most of the fishermen waiting did not have this philosophical attitude.

A friend of mine, John de Cubelis, was fishing one day with spinning tackle using a dacron line. He had found a spot where there were plenty of Stripers and they were biting. But, despite the fact that John is an expert fisherman, every Bass he hooked broke his line before he could land him. Finally John made a discovery. Due to the short three inch loop he was using to attach the swivel and leader to the line, the dacron line was breaking. The short loop was causing the line to fray against the swivel and thereby weaken, so as soon as he had a fighting fish on, the line broke. He substituted a ten inch loop tied with a barrel or jimmie knot; the line held and he caught Bass.

I predict that with the improvements in spinning tackle that are bound to come, this method of fishing will become so popular that it will eventually replace all but fly rods and bait casting rods for inshore fishing. The glass spinning rod is fast surpassing spinning rods made of other material. However, due to difference in manufacturing, the rods vary to some degree in weight, so it is best to consider the length of the rod rather than the weight when purchasing one.

At present writing, the monofilament line leads the field but the dacron line, and others, are fast developing into stiff

competition. Regarding the monofilament line, do not be mis-
lead by its test. A 6 to 10 pound test monofilament line on a
light spinning rod, will stand a far greater strain than is indicated. To verify this statement, place a three-pound weight on
the floor, run the line through the guides of the rod and attach
it to the weight. Then, holding the rod at the eleven o'clock
position (the correct position) slowly try raising the weight from
the floor. You will find that the rod and line stand the strain
despite the fact that it will tax your strength to lift the weight.

The present spinning reel will not stand salt water without
"freezing" unless well-oiled and greased. Since the mechanism
is simple, the reel is easily taken apart and re-assembled; there
is no excuse for not caring for it properly.

Spinning Tackle

The tackle herewith listed is the gear that is best suited
for the beginner and the average angler. It does not cover
the complete field of spinning equipment.

BLACK SEA BASS

Tackle—

Rod: 5 to 6 ft. glass or beryllium copper.
Reel: 100 to 200 yard.
Line: 6 to 12 lb. test monofilament.
Leader: none.
Lures: none.
Sinker: 1 to 2 oz.
Hooks: Leader hooks No. 2 to 5 having a 10 to 12 in. leader
of nylon or gut.

Bait—Sea clams, squid and quahogs.

Method—Bottom fishing from boat.

For surf fishing use the same tackle with the exception of
the rod being 6 to 12 ft. long, the sinkers 1 to 3 oz.

BLUEFISH

Tackle—

Rod: 4 to 6 ft. glass or beryllium copper.
Reel: 100 to 200 yard.
Line: 8 to 12 lb. test monofilament.
Leader: stainless steel cable or wire 10 to 24 in.
Lures: small feathers or plugs.
Sinker: 1 to 3 oz.
Hooks: 2/0 to 4/0.

BAIT—Worms, mullet, squid and soft shell clams.

METHOD—Trolling from a boat or free line fishing with no sinker and chum with menhaden or mackerel. No sinker.

For surf fishing use the same tackle with the exception of the rod being 6 to 12 feet and leader 6 to 18 in. No lures.

BONITA

Not fished for to date to any extent with spin tackle.

CHANNEL BASS (REDFISH)

TACKLE—

Rod: 6 to 8 ft. glass or bamboo.
Reel: 200 yard.
Line: 12 lb. test monofilament.
Leader: not necessary.
Lures: small feathers, eelskin, plugs or spoons.
Sinker: 1 to 3 oz.
Hooks: Leader hooks 4/0 to 7/0 with 6 to 18 in. nylon or gut leader.

BAIT—mullet, squid and shedder crabs.

METHOD—Trolling from boat. No sinker. Leader optional.

For surf fishing use the same tackle with the exception of the rod being 6 to 12 ft. glass. Leader hooks take place of a leader.

COD FISH

TACKLE—

Rod: 6 ft. glass.
Reel: 100 to 200 yard.
Line: 4 to 12 lb. test monofilament.
Leader: 6 to 18 in. nylon or gut.
Lures: none.
Sinker: 1 to 3 oz.
Hooks: 4/0 to 7/0.

BAIT—sea claims, squid and quahogs.

METHOD—Bottom fishing from boat. Spin fishing is not recommended for a party boat. No fishing from shore.

EELS

Spinning tackle is too light to handle eels of any size.

FLATFISH (WINTER FLOUNDER)

TACKLE—
   Rod: 5 to 6 ft. glass, bamboo or beryllium copper.
   Reel: 100 yard.
   Line: 4 to 8 lb. test monofilament.
   Leader: 6 to 12 in. nylon or gut.
   Lures: none.
   Sinker: ½ to 1 oz.
   Hooks: 8 to 10 Chestertown.
BAIT—worms (blood and sand) and clam bits.
METHOD—Bottom fishing from boat. Bait fishing.

For surf fishing use the same tackle with the exception of the rod being 6 to 12 ft. glass. Line, 8 to 12 lb. test monofilament. Sinkers, 1 to 3 oz. Reel, 100 to 200 yard.

FLUKE (SUMMER FLOUNDER)

TACKLE—
   Rod: 4 to 6 ft. glass, bamboo, beryllium copper.
   Reel: 100 to 200 yard.
   Line: 6 to 12 lb. test monofilament.
   Leader: 6 to 12 in. nylon or gut.
   Lures: none.
   Sinker: 1 to 2 oz.
   Hooks: 2/0 to 4/0.
BAIT—shiners, chubs, mummies and squid.
METHOD—Bottom fishing from boat. Bait fishing.

For surf fishing use the same tackle with the exception of the rod being 6 to 12 ft. glass or bamboo. Line, 8 to 12 lb. test monofilament. Sinker, 1 to 3 oz.

KINGFISH

TACKLE—
   Rod: 6 to 12 ft. glass, bamboo or beryllium copper.
   Reel: 100 yard.
   Line: 6 to 12 lb. test monofilament.
   Leader: none.
   Lures: none.
   Sinker: 1 to 3 oz.
   Hooks: Leader hooks, number 1/0 with 6 to 18 in. gut or
       nylon leader.
BAIT—big shrimps, worms and soft shell crabs.
METHOD—Bottom fishing, surf.

MACKEREL

TACKLE—
Rod: 4 to 6 ft. glass, bamboo or beryllium copper.
Reel: 100 yard.
Line: 4 to 6 lb. test monofilament.
Leader: none.
Lures: small feathers, flies, streamers or spoons.
Sinker: none.

BAIT—none.

METHOD—Trolling from boat. Surf fishing.

POLLACK

TACKLE—
Rod: 4 to 12 ft. glass, bamboo or beryllium copper.
Reel: 100 to 200 yard.
Line: 8 to 12 lb. test monofilament.
Leader: none.
Lures: small feathers, plugs.
Sinker: none.

BAIT—none.

METHOD—From surf. To date not done to any appreciable extent from a boat.

POMPANO

TACKLE—
Rod: 4 to 8 ft. glass.
Reel: 100 yard.
Line: 6 to 12 lb. test monofilament.
Leader: 6 to 12 in. nylon or gut.
Lures: small feathers or streamers.
Sinker: none.
Hooks: Leader hooks, 2/0 to 6/0 having a 6 to 12 in. leader of nylon or gut.

BAIT—sand fleas, mullet and big shrimp.

METHOD—Troll or cast from a boat.

For surf fishing use the same tackle with the exception of the rod being 6 to 12 ft. long.

PORGY or SCUP

TACKLE—
Rod: 4 to 8 ft. glass.
Reel: 100 yard.

Line: 6 to 12 lb. test monofilament.
Leader: none.
Lures: none.
Sinker: 1 to 4 oz.
Hooks: Leader hooks, number 2 to 4 having a nylon or
   tarred line leader 6 to 12 in.

BAIT—worms, sea clams and squid.

METHOD—Bottom fishing from boat, surf fishing.

SAILFISH

TACKLE—
   Rod: 6 to 8 ft. glass.
   Reel: 200 to 300 yard.
   Line: 12 lb. test monofilament.
   Leader: 3 to 15 ft. stainless steel cable or nylon.
   Lures: none.
   Sinker: none.
   Hooks: 5/0 to 8/0.

BAIT—whole mullet and mullet strips.

METHOD—From boat only. A drail should be used on at least
   one line that is overboard.

SHAD

TACKLE—
   Rod: 4 to 10 ft. glass or bamboo.
   Reel: 100 yard.
   Line: 4 to 8 lb. test monofilament.
   Leader: none.
   Lures: small feathers, flies or spinners.
   Sinker: add weight if necessary.
   Hooks: none.

BAIT—none.

METHOD—Surf casting.

SHARK

Do not recommend the use of Spinning tackle for this fish.

SNAPPER BLUES

TACKLE—
   Rod: 4 to 8 ft. glass.
   Reel: 100 yard.
   Line: 4 to 6 lb. test monofilament.

Leader: none.

Lures: flies, streamers or small spoons.

Sinker: none.

Hooks: Leader hooks, number 4 long shank Snapper having a nylon or gut leader of 12 in.

BAIT—shiners and mummies.

METHOD—Casting from boat, or shore.

STRIPED BASS

TACKLE—

Rod: 6 to 8 ft. glass, bamboo or beryllium copper.

Reel: 100 to 300 yard.

Line: 8 to 12 lb. test monofilament.

Leader: none.

Lure: small feathers, spinner with worms, plugs or eelskin.

Sinker: none. Or 1 to 3 oz. for surf.

Hooks: 2/0 to 6/0 for surf.

BAIT—worms, squid, soft shell crabs and menhaden.

METHOD—Trolling or casting from boat.

For surf fishing use the same tackle with the exception of the rod being 6 to 12 ft. Leader of nylon, gut or wire 6 to 18 in. used.

TARPON

TACKLE—

Rod: 4 to 8 ft. glass, bamboo or beryllium copper.

Reel: 200 to 300 yard.

Line: 8 to 12 lb. test monofilament.

Leader: 6 to 15 ft. stainless steel cable or wire.

Lures: streamers or plugs

Sinker: add weight necessary.

Hooks: Leader hooks, 4/0 to 8/0 having cable leader 12 to 18 in. for surf, bottom.

BAIT—mullet and pin fish.

METHOD—Trolling from boat.

For surf fishing, bottom or casting, use the same tackle with the exception of the rod being 4 to 10 ft. Lures, plugs, feathers or spoons. Leader not necessary. No sinker.

TAUTOG (BLACKFISH)

TACKLE—

Rod: 4 to 8 ft. glass, bamboo or beryllium copper.

Reel: 100 yard.

Line: 8 to 12 lb. test monofilament.
Leader: none.
Lures: none.
Sinker: 2 to 5 oz. 1 to 3 oz. for surf.
Hooks: Leader hooks, number 2 to 5 having leaders of
    tarred line, nylon or gut, 12 in.
BAIT—fiddler crabs, green crabs and sea clams.
METHOD—Bottom fishing from boat.

For surf bottom fishing use the same tackle with the exception
of the rod being 4 to 9 ft. Use the lighter sinkers.

TUNA (BLUEFIN)

The light spinning tackle is out of the question.

TUNA ("SCHOOL")

Not fished for to date to any extent with spin tackle.

WEAKFISH (SPOTTED TROUT, SEA TROUT)

TACKLE—
Rod: 4 to 8 ft. glass, bamboo or beryllium copper.
Reel: 100 yard.
Line: 6 to 12 lb. test monofilament.
Leader: 12 to 18 in. nylon or cable.
Lures: small feathers or spinners.
Sinker: none. 1 to 3 oz. surf.
Hooks: Leader hooks, number 2 to 5 having nylon, cable or
    gut leaders 12 to 18 in.
BAIT—blood worms, sand worms, squid.
METHOD—Trolling and free line from a boat.

For surf fishing, casting or bottom use the same tackle with
the exception of the rod being 4 to 10 ft., the reel 100 to 200
yard, use 1 to 3 oz. sinkers. Cable leader, nylon or gut.

SEASON, PLACE, TACKLE AND HOW

The tackle herewith listed is the gear that is best suited for
the beginner and the average angler. It does not cover the
complete field of fishing equipment.

BLACK SEA BASS

SEASON—May through October.
WHERE—Florida to Maine in bays, over mussel beds, rocks and
    wrecks. Bottom fishing.

TACKLE—Regular boat rod, 18 in. butt, and 5 ft. tip of 5 to 10 ounces, 100 yard reel, 10 to 20 lb. test line, 1/0 to 4/0 Sproat hooks, 12 inch gut or nylon leader and 2 to 5 oz. sinker.

BAIT—Sea clams, squid, skimmers, worms, and soft crabs.

TIME—Incoming tide is best.

PREPARE—Skin then fry or bake. Very good eating.

BLUEFISH

SEASON—May into November.

WHERE—Florida to Maine in bay channels, surf and offshore. Trolling, surf casting or jigging.

TACKLE—Fishing from boat—Regular boat rod, 18 in. butt, 5 ft. tip of 5 to 10 oz., 200 yard reel, 20 to 36 lb. test line, 4/0 to 6/0 O'Shaughnessey hooks, 3 ft. stainless steel cable or wire and ½ to 10 ounce sinker.

BAIT—Blood and sandworms, squid, bunker, feathers or spoon.

TIME—High tide or at times any tide.

PREPARE—Scale, fillet or bake whole after cleaning. Excellent eating. Can also be broiled and fried.

SURF FISHING—Same tackle as above except use surf rod with 30 in. butt and 7 ft. tip of 10 to 16 oz. The same bait.

BONITA

SEASON—July to October.

WHERE—Carolinas to Maine. Offshore, rarely inshore. Trolling.

TACKLE—Regular boat rod, 18 in. butt, 5 ft. tip, 6 to 10 oz., 150 to 200 yard reel, 36 to 45 lb. test line, 3/0 to 6/0 hooks, 15 to 24 inch leader of stainless steel or piano wire.

BAIT—Artificial lures.

TIME—All day.

PREPARE—Seldom eaten but can be cut in steaks, baked or fried.

CHANNEL BASS (REDFISH)

SEASON—May through October.

WHERE—South Carolina to New Jersey in inlets, over bars with breaking surf. Surf casting, trolling, top and bottom.

TACKLE—Fishing from boat—Regular boat rod, 18 in. butt, 5 ft. tip of 5 to 10 ounces, 200 yard reel, 36 to 45 lb. test line, 6/0 to 9/0 O'Shaughnessey hooks, 15 inch nylon, gut or wire leader and 1 to 10 ounce sinkers.

BAIT—Mullet, soft shell crabs, squid and eels.

TIME—Half tide to full tide is best.

PREPARE—Scale, then cut into steaks and bake. Not popular eating.

For shore fishing use the same tackle except for a surf rod with 30 inch butt and 7 ft. tip of 10 to 16 ounces. The same bait.

CODFISH

SEASON—The year round.

WHERE—New Jersey to Nova Scotia offshore in deep water over reefs, rocks and wrecks. Closer in to shore during the spring and fall. Bottom fishing.

TACKLE—Regular boat rod, 18 in. butt, 5 ft. tip 12 to 16 ounces, 200 yard reel, 35 to 46 pound test line, 6/0 to 8/0 Sproat hooks, 7/0 gut leader and 4 to 12 ounce sinker.

BAIT—Squid, clams, worms and conch.

TIME—First three hours of incoming tide are best.

PREPARE—Cut into steaks, bake whole or fry. Very good eating.

EELS

SEASON—The year round.

WHERE—Florida to Nova Scotia along coast line, bays and rivers. Bottom fish or spear.

TACKLE—Hand line, 15 to 20 pound test, eel spear, 2/0 to 6/0 hooks and 3 to 8 ounce sinker.

BAIT—Squid, worms, shiners, chub minnows and soft crabs.

TIME—Night time.

PREPARE—Skin then fry or pickle in vinegar for later use.

Fishing for Eel's is not done frequently with a rod and reel, but should the angler decide to try it, use a regular boat rod with 10 to 16 ounce tip, 100 to 200 yard reel, 20 to 45 lb. test line, 18 inch leader of gut or nylon and 2/0 to 6/0 hooks. Same bait.

FLATFISH (WINTER FLOUNDER)

SEASON—March to December.

WHERE—New Jersey to Maine in bays and off the shore line. Bottom fishing.

TACKLE—Regular boat rod, 18 in. butt, 5 ft. tip, 5 to 10 ounces, 100 yard reel, 10 to 20 pound test line, 8 to 10 Chestertown hooks, 10 inch nylon or gut leader with spreader and 1 to 5 ounce sinker.

BAIT—Blood and sandworms, clams and black mussels.

TIME—High tide is the best.

PREPARE—Fillet or fry. Very good eating.

FLUKE (SUMMER FLOUNDER)

SEASON—May to October.

WHERE—Florida to Maine in bays, channels, inlets, under bridges, in weed beds, surf and offshore. Bottom fishing, drifting and casting.

TACKLE—From a boat—Regular boat rod, 18 in. butt, 5 ft. tip of 5 to 10 ounces, 100 to 150 yard reel, 18 to 30 lb. test line, 2/0 to 4/0 Carlisle hooks, 18 to 20 inch nylon or gut leader and 1 to 5 ounce sinker.

BAIT—Squid, worms, live killies and shiners.

TIME—High tide is the best.

PREPARE—Fillet or fry. Very good eating.

SURF FISHING—Surf rod with 30 inch butt, 7 foot tip, 10 to 16 ounces, 150 to 200 yard reel, 20 to 36 pound test line, 2/0 to 4/0 Carlisle hooks and 12 to 30 inch gut or nylon leader.

KINGFISH

SEASON—May to November.

WHERE—From the Carolinas to Massachusetts off sandy bottoms, in bays and inlets. Bottom fishing.

TACKLE—Regular boat rod, 18 in. butt, 5 ft. tip, 5 to 10 ounces, 150 to 200 yard reel, 18 to 36 pound test line, 1/0 to 3/0 Sproat hooks, 15 to 24 inch gut or nylon leader and 1 to 5 ounce sinkers.

BAIT—Shrimp, blood or sandworms.

TIME—The two hours of the incoming tide up to full tide.

PREPARE—Scale, then bake or fry. Excellent eating.

MACKEREL

SEASON—June to November.

WHERE—Cape May to Maine in deep water, inlets and along shore. Trolling, casting, chumming and float fishing.

TACKLE—Regular bait casting rod, 5 or 6 feet, overall, 5 to 10 ounce tip, or a 5 to 6 ounce fly rod, 100 yard reel, 10 to 20 pound test line, 1/0 to 3/0 O'Shaughnessey hooks, 12 to 36 inch nylon or gut leader, wire and ½ to 1 ounce sinkers.

BAIT—Portions of mackerel, squid, bloodworms and spinner lure.

TIME—Not greatly influenced by the tides.

PREPARE—Scale, then best broiled or baked whole. Excellent eating.

POLLACK (BOSTON BLUES)

SEASON—The year round.

WHERE—Nova Scotia to Cape May, over rocky bottoms, off breakwaters and in inlets. Bottom fishing during the winter, trolling during spring, summer and fall.

TACKLE—Regular boat rod, 18 in. butt, 5 ft. tip of 5 to 10 oz., 200 yard reel, 36 to 45 lb. test line, 5/0 to 7/0 O'Shaughnessey hooks, wire, gut or nylon leader 18 in. and 3 to 10 ounce sinkers.

BAIT—See clams or squid for bottom feeding. Feathers or lead squid for trolling.

TIME—One hour before and during the turn of the tide.

PREPARE—Skin, cut into steaks and then bake whole or fry. Very good eating.

POMPANO

SEASON—The year round in southern waters.

WHERE—Florida southward in open water and bays. Bottom fishing and trolling.

TACKLE—Bait casting rod or medium boat rod, 100 to 150 yard reel, 20 to 36 lb. test line, 2/0 to 4/0 hooks, steel wire, nylon or gut leader of 18 to 24 inches and 3 to 10 oz. sinker.

BAIT—Sand fleas and shrimp.

TIME—The last two hours of the incoming tide are best.

PREPARE—Scale then fry, bake or broil. Excellent eating.

PORGY or SCUP

SEASON—May through October.

WHERE—Cape May to Maine over mussel beds, sandy bottoms and rocks. Bottom fishing.

TACKLE—Regular boat rod, 18 in. butt, 5 ft. tip, 5 to 10 oz., 100 yard reel, 10 to 20 pound test line, 1 to 4 Sproat hooks, 12 inch gut or nylon leader and 1 to 5 oz. sinkers.

BAIT—Worms, squid, skimmers, shrimp and soft clams.

TIME—No choice of tides.

PREPARE—Scale, then fry or bake. Good eating.

SAILFISH

SEASON—The year round in southern waters.

WHERE—Florida southward in open water. Trolling.

TACKLE—A regular boat rod of 6 to 14 ounce tip, 200 to 400 yard reel, 36 to 72 lb. test line, 5/0 to 8/0 hooks, 2 ft. to 5 ft. leader of steel wire, nylon or gut.

BAIT—Whole mullet or strips of dolphin.

TIME—From half tide to full tide.

PREPARE—Caught for the sport of it, not eaten—thrown back.

SHAD

SEASON—May to November.

WHERE—New Jersey to Maine in rivers, inlets from shore. Top fishing. Fly fishing, bait casting and surf casting.

TACKLE—Fly rod of 5 to 6 ounces, surf rod, bait casting rod 4 to 6 ft. over all, 100 yard reel, 12 to 20 pound test line, 2/0 O'Shaugnessey hook and stainless steel or nylon leader 12 to 24 inches.

BAIT—Feathers or spinner.

TIME—High tide.

PREPARE—Fillet, fry, broil or bake. Good eating.

SHARK

SEASON—July to October.

WHERE—Off the northern Atlantic shore, in deep water offshore; off beaches near inlets, over rocky formations. Bottom fishing; drifting and harpooning.

TACKLE—Heavy regular boat rod, 18 in. butt, 5 ft. tip of 20 to 36 ounces, 400 to 600 yard reel, 45 to 54 pound test line, 9/0 to 12/0 (or larger) hooks and 15 ft. stainless steel cable or piano wire leader.

BAIT—Whole fish.

TIME—Outgoing tide in inlets, incoming tide offshore.

PREPARE—Cut into steaks, broil or bake. Good eating.

SNAPPER BLUES

SEASON—August to October.

WHERE—Maine to Cape May. Long Island Sound. In bays and inlets. Top fishing, cast or troll. Chum used.

TACKLE—Fly rod of 5 to 6 ounces, bait casting rod of 4 to 6 ft. over all, 100 yard reel, 10 to 18 pound test line, 1 to 4 longshank Snapper hooks, 12 to 15 inch nylon or wire leader.

BAIT—Killies, shiners, small spinner and flys.

TIME—Incoming tide.

PREPARE—Scale then broil or fry. Excellent eating.

STRIPED BASS (ROCKFISH)

SEASON—April through November.
WHERE—Cape May to Maine. Long Island Sound. In surf, inlets and bays. Bottom fishing, surf casting or troll. Chum.
TACKLE—Fishing from boat—Regular boat rod, 18 in. butt, 5 ft. tip of 5 to 10 ounces, 150 yard reel, 20 to 45 pound test line, 5/0 to 7/0 O'Shaughnessey hooks, 24 inch wire, nylon or gut leader and 1 to 6 ounce sinkers.
BAIT—Sand or bloodworms, softshell crabs, squid, menhaden and plugs.
TIME—From dusk until dawn.
PREPARE—Scale then bake or fry. Excellent eating.

For surf fishing use a surf rod with 30 inch butt, 7 ft. tip of from 10 to 16 ounces, 200 yard reel, 20 to 45 lb. test line, hooks and sinkers same as for boat fishing. The same bait.

TARPON

SEASON—The year round in southern waters.
WHERE—Florida southward, in open water, bays and rivers. Trolling and casting.
TACKLE—Bait casting rod, 5 to 6 ft. over all, or, 6 to 14 ounce boat rod, 200 to 400 yard reel, 12 to 45 lb. test line, 4/0 to 8/0 hooks, steel wire, nylon or gut leader 18 in. to 3 ft.
BAIT—Mullet and plugs.
TIME—From half to full tide.
PREPARE—Seldom eaten.

TAUTOG (BLACKFISH)

SEASON—April through November.
WHERE—New Jersey to Nova Scotia in bays, over rocky bottoms, pilings and wrecks and offshore. Bottom fishing.
TACKLE—Regular boat rod, 18 in. butt, 5 ft. tip of 5 to 10 oz., 150 yard reel, 36 to 45 pound test line, number 3 to 5 tarred line snelled hooks (Virginia), and 1 to 6 oz. sinkers.
BAIT—Worms, fiddler or green crabs, Hermit crabs, sea clams and skimmers.
TIME—Along shore at high tide; other places, incoming half tide.
PREPARE—Skin then broil or fry. Excellent eating.

TUNA (BLUEFIN, GREAT)

SEASON—May until late October.

WHERE—Newfoundland to Florida. Offshore, Troll and chum.

TACKLE—Heavy boat rod, 21 inch butt, 6 ft. 9 inch tip of 36 oz., 800 to 1600 yard reel, 117 to 216 pound test line, 10/0 to 14/0 Sobey or Grinnell hooks and 15 ft. stainless steel cable or wire leader.

BAIT—Whole butterfish, mackerel, whiting and herring.

TIME—High tide is best.

PREPARE—Cut into steaks then broil or bake. Good eating.

TUNA ("SCHOOL")

SEASON—July through September.

WHERE—Newfoundland to Florida. Trolling or chum.

TACKLE—Regular boat rod, 18 in. butt, 5 ft. tip of 16 oz., 150 to 200 yard reel, 25 to 36 pound test line, 5/0 to 8/0 Sobey or O'Shaughnessey hooks and 18 inch to 5 ft. stainless steel cable or wire leader.

BAIT—Squid and feather lure.

TIME—Not influenced by tides—just find them.

PREPARE—Cut into steaks then bake or broil. Good eating.

WEAKFISH (SPOTTED TROUT, SEA TROUT)

SEASON—May to November.

WHERE—Florida to the Virginia Capes. Comparatively few come into the more northern waters. Bottom fishing, trolling, free line or surf casting. Chum.

TACKLE—Fishing from boat—Regular boat rod, 18 in. butt, 5 ft. tip of 3 or 4 ounces, 150 to 200 yard reel, 20 to 45 lb. test line, 2/0 to 4/0 Sproat hooks, 3 ft. nylon or gut leader and 2 to 6 ounce sinkers.

BAIT—Blood or sandworms, shrimp, squid, soft shell clams, small plugs, wood block, jigs and feathers.

TIME—Outgoing tide in inlets and bays, incoming tide in open water.

PREPARE—Scale, skin or fillet then bake, broil or fry. Excellent eating.

For surf fishing use a regular surf rod, 200 yard reel, and 25 to 45 pound test line. The same hooks and leader as for boat fishing. The same bait.

CHAPTER V

※

Baits

THE SEA WORM is undoubtedly the most popular bait used along the Atlantic seaboard. Sea Worms are dug up in various localities but the majority of them come from the coast of Maine and are shipped to all points. They stay alive for a considerable length of time and are easy to ship and handle. They are sold in most tackle shops.

BLOOD WORMS
(Glycera dibranchiata; Glycera americana)
(Genus: *Glycera*)

BLOODWORM

The Blood Worm is also called the White Worm, Four-Jawed Worm, Proboscis Worm and Beak Thrower. It is from six to eight inches in length with a round, smooth body, narrow, faintly visible segments tapering at either end. Its color varies from light pink to red and it frequently has a purplish tinge. When disturbed, the Blood Worm flicks out a long proboscis that has on its end four tiny jaws, black in color. It is found in the mud flats along the Atlantic coast from Maine to the Carolinas. To most fish the Blood Worm is a very palatable food.

CLAM WORMS
(Genus: *Nereis*)

The Clam Worm is the most numerous of all the worms found along the Atlantic coast, from Labrador to South Carolina. It has a rounded body and flat underside. Its dark, prismatic back, varying from reddish brown to blue or green in color, has distinct segments throughout its length. The underside, pink, red or orange in color, has two rows of appendages that are used for swimming and breathing. These appendages

CLAM WORM

give the Clam Worm a slight resemblance to the familiar thousand legger. The average length of this worm is from five to ten inches but the *Nereis virens* attains the length of some eighteen inches.

The *Nereis virens* prefers muddy and shelly sand into which it burrows, but it can also be found under rocks midway between the low and high tide water marks. It emerges from its burrow at night to lie along the flats or swim in shallow water. This species has black jaws and feeds on other worms. A popular bait, the *Nereis virens* is generally sold under the name of Sand Worm.

A smaller species, the *Nereis limbata*, is also often called the Sand Worm. It attains a length of about six inches and has yellow jaws instead of black. It prefers a more sandy soil than do most worms.

A third species of the *Nereis* family is the *Nereis pelagica*. This worm is not used as generally for bait as are the other two species. Reddish brown in color, with its middle the widest part of its body, it is found under stones, on shell bottoms and among mussels. The male is about seven inches long, the female about five. It is most numerous northward of Cape Cod. The Clam worm, like the Blood Worm, is taken by most fish. In some sections it is called the Much Worm.

Lug Worm
(Genus: *Arenicola marina*)

The Lug Worm is black, brownish or olive in color with a rough skin that is covered with tuft-like hairy gills. It enjoys the questionable distinction of being the ugliest of the worms that are used for bait. Also called the Burrowing Worm, it has a head nearly twice as thick as the rest of its body and it gives

LUG WORM

forth a yellowish liquid which qualifies it as a messy bait to handle. The species most commonly found is *Arenicola marina*. Ranging southward from Rhode Island, it lives in U-shaped burrows in mud and sand flats. These burrows can be located by piles of castings around the two entrances to the burrow. Generally, at low tide the worm emerges from its home to crawl about on the ground. The Lug Worm averages about eight inches in length, but attains some twelve inches, and, despite its appearance, it is liked by fish.

Ribbon Worm
(*Cerebratulus lacteus*)
(Genus: *Cerebratulus*)

RIBBON WORM

The Ribbon Worm is sometimes called the Proboscis Worm or the Tape Worm. This last name is misleading; the worm is in no way related to the Tape Worm which, on occasion, troubles man and animals.

This worm lives in mud and sand near the low water mark and is easily recognized by its long, flat body, which in some species can attain a twenty foot length. It is of a yellowish-white or pinkish in color, and, like the Blood Worm, can shoot out a proboscis from its head. Being very fragile, this worm must be handled with care, as it breaks into pieces very easily. The species most commonly found along the Atlantic coast from Maine to Florida is *Cerebratulus lacteus*. Practically all fish are fond of it.

CLAMS

SURF CLAM

(Genus, *Mactra solidissima; Spisula solidissima*)

Known also as the Giant Clam, Hen Clam, Sea Clam, Skimmer Clam and Ocean Clam, it is the largest along the Atlantic coast. It is found from North Carolina to Labrador, being most

SURF CLAM

numerous in New England waters down to New Jersey. The Surf Clam reaches a measurement of about seven inches and is of yellowish-white, brown or light gray in color. It has a very heavy shell and a powerful foot with which it digs into the sand. It lives in the surf along the ocean-front and is also found in water of fifty to sixty feet in depth.

A somewhat smaller variety inhabits southern waters, south from Cape Hatteras.

The Surf Clam is located by wading into shallow water or after a storm it is often found washed up on the beach.

This bivalve mollusk is a close second in popularity as bait and is sold by all bait and tackle stores. Well-liked by fish.

Hard Shell Clam

(Genus: *Venus mercenaria*)

This is the common Clam of the Atlantic coast that is ordered in restaurants and hotels. It is also called the Round Clam, Cherrystone Clam, Little-neck Clam and Quahog depending on its size and the locality.

HARD SHELL CLAM

The Hard Shell Clam, fully grown, may attain six inches in measurement but the average run is about three inches or less. In color it is white, gray or yellowish on the outside with a violet border on the inside edge of the shell. Found from Florida to Maine in muddy and sandy bottoms of bays, sounds and inlets, it is always on sale in fish markets and in shops along the roadside that specialize in Clams. These Clams are liked by nearly all fish.

Soft Shell Clam

(Genus: *Mya arenaria*)

This Clam is also known by other names such as Soft Clam, Nannynose, Steamer Clam, Long-neck Clam and Squirt Clam, to name a few. It may measure as much as five inches, but generally it averages from two to three inches. It is easily identified by its long neck and oval-shaped shell, which is of a dull gray or a chalky white in color. Ranging from the Arctic seas to North Carolina, the Soft Shell Clam is found in greatest numbers north of Cape Cod. It lives in muddy bottoms, usually buried a foot or so below the surface between the low and high

SOFT SHELL CLAM

water marks. It is easily detected on the mud flats, for it squirts water into the air as a person walks over the area where it is located. This water is jetted from the neck which is, in reality, a syphon. They can also be dug up with a garden fork in the tidal flats. Being a food desired by fish, most roadside dealers and fish markets carry the Soft Shell Clam for sale.

MUSSELS

These bivalves are found clinging to piles, rocks and any other objects that are below the high water mark in bays or the ocean. They may be of several colors: blue-black, olive, brown or black, depending on the species.

EDIBLE MUSSEL *(Mytilus edilus)*

Along the Atlantic shore, where it ranges from the Arctic to North Carolina, the most common Mussel is the Edible Mussel. Its largest measurement is about three inches with the

EDIBLE MUSSEL

average being from one inch to two and a half inches. Besides being used for bait, this Mussel can be crushed and used for chum. Also known as the Atlantic Mussel, Blue Mussel and Sea Mussel, it is sold by most bait and tackle shops.

RIBBED MUSSEL (*Modiolus demissus plicatulus*)

This mussel is also quite common to the Atlantic coast and is known also as the Fan Mussel or Mudbank Mussel. It has a

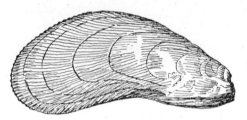

RIBBED MUSSEL

dull brownish or olive-ribbed shell and attains a measurement of three inches, the average, however, being much smaller. It is a good bait and is also used, crushed, to make chum. Bait shops generally carry it.

SCALLOPS

While this shellfish is used more for food than for fishing, the soft portion of the meat can be used successfully for bait for the same fish that like clams and mussels.

There are two kinds of Scallops: the Sea Scallop (*Pecten grandis*) the largest, which is found in the ocean from New

SCALLOP

Jersey to Labrador and the smaller kind (*Pecten irradian*) which inhabits inshore waters from Florida to New England.

The best way to obtain Scallops for fishing is to locate a place where the commercial Scallop fishermen come to shore after a catch. Here they remove the heavy muscle which holds the two Scallop shells together and which is served in restaurants. The shells are then discarded and there is sufficient meat left in them—the soft portion—to provide you with your Scallop bait. And this can generally be had without charge.

SNAILS, WHELKS, CONCHS

Moon Snail (*Palinices heros*)

There are a number of species of the Moon Snail along the Atlantic coast, among the largest is the *Polinices heros.* It is identified by the typical snail shell and a meaty foot which extends beyond the shell. From the Gulf of the Saint Lawrence to North Carolina, it is found, wholly or partially buried in

MOON SNAIL

sand or mud between the low and high water marks, in shallow water and also in water to more than 1200 feet in depth. When fully grown this snail is about four inches across. A close relative, the Sand or Collar Snail, (*Polinices duplicata*) which is not quite as large, is found as far south as Florida and the Gulf of Mexico.

The meaty portion of these snails is tough, and, cut up, can be used for many bottom feeding fish. It is a bait that is not easily stolen by Cunners (Bergalls).

Periwinkle (*Littorina litorea*)

The common or edible Periwinkle is the small sea snail that is so numerous in seaweed in shallow water and is found clinging to piles and rocks and also along the beach between the low and high water marks. It is found from Delaware Bay to

Labrador but is most numerous along the New England shores where it prefers rocky areas.

This little snail is also called Shore Periwinkle or Winkle. It has the typical snail shell which is colored black, yellowish-

EDIBLE PERIWINKLE

brown, olive-green or gray with brown bands. While definitely on the small side, the Periwinkle shell can be cracked and the meat extracted. And when several pieces are strung together on a hook they make good bait.

WHELKS

The meat of the Whelks makes a good bait for bottom fishing as it is very tough and not easily stolen by Bergalls or Cunners. However, since few bait shops carry Whelks as a general practice, the angler has to go after them himself using wire traps baited with dead fish which are set out at night.

The Whelks are the largest univalve shells found north of Cape Hatteras in Atlantic waters. There are several groups, three of which are most generally used for bait. The Whelk is particularly relished by Codfish.

The Waved Whelk (*Buccinum undatum*) is found from New Jersey to Labrador. It is a brownish color and averages from two to four inches in length. It stays close to shore in its northern range, out in deep water in its southern.

The Channeled Whelk (*Busycon canaliculatum*) ranges from northern Florida to Cape Cod. Also known as Conch or Winkle, it attains a length of from six to nine inches. It prefers shallow, sandy bottoms.

The Knobbed Whelk (*Busycon caricum*) also known as the

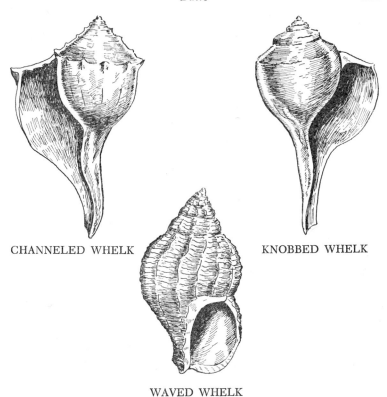

CHANNELED WHELK   KNOBBED WHELK

WAVED WHELK

Giant Whelk or Pear Conch is the largest Whelk of the Atlantic coast. It reaches a length of some ten inches and is also distinguished by a row of knobs near the top of the shell. It is found from Florida to Cape Cod.

There are numerous other species of Whelk all of which are suitable for bait. The meat can be used intact or cut into smaller pieces for bottom fishing.

SQUID

The common Atlantic Squid (*Loligo pealii*), also called Inkfish and Blunt-tailed Squid, is found along the Atlantic from South Carolina to Massachusetts from the shore line to water fifty fathoms deep. Its round body, tapering off to a tail, aver-

ages from five to eight inches in length. On the end of the tail
are two horizontal fins. The head contains two large, staring
eyes and ten tentacles that substitute for a nose. Two of these
tentacles, larger and longer than the others, trail back along
the sides of the head and body. The tentacles hide a parrot-
like beak which constitutes the mouth.

The common Squid, becoming rare north of Cape Cod, is
replaced by the Short-tailed Squid (*Omastrephes illecebrosas*)

COMMON SQUID

also called Sea Arrow, or Flying Squid. This Squid has shorter
fins and is usually found in deep water.

Several other species of Squid abound in the Atlantic,
ranging from two inches to approximately fifty feet, the Giant
Squid.

The Squid is seldom used alive as bait due to the fact that
it is difficult to keep in captivity. A tough bait, used whole
or cut into strips for smaller fish, the meat is tough and will
remain on a hook for a considerable length of time if properly
placed.

CRABS

Blue Crab (*Caloinectus sapidus*)

The most popular crab along the Atlantic coast used for
bait is the Blue Crab in the Shedder stage—also called Sea
Crab, Blueclaw Crab or Common Edible Crab. It is found from
Florida to Cape Cod and is recognized by its comparatively
large size—six inches across the top shell—and by its coloration.
It has a green back, white belly and long claws which are
bright blue blending into a red at the tips. Being a swimming
crab, its hind legs are paddle-shaped.

The Blue Crab is found in salt and brackish waters in bays,
inlets, sounds and rivers. Here it seeks muddy bottoms preferably covered with eel grass or sea lettuce. From May to
October it remains in shallow water, but with the coming of
cold weather it moves to deep water.

Commercial fishermen, bait dealers and fish markets sell the Blue Crab in both the hard and soft shell stages. Nevertheless, many anglers prefer to catch their own by means of crab traps

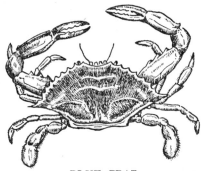

BLUE CRAB

or crab nets used from a boat. Another method is to fasten a fish head on a line, lower it into the water, and when the crab takes hold of it slowly ease him out of the water and into a net.

LADY CRAB (*Ovalipes oscellatus*)

The Lady Crab is found along sandy beaches and inlets from Florida to Cape Cod. It is particularly suited as bait for surf fishing. The shell, somewhat circular in shape, is about three inches in length and width and is yellow with reddish or purplish spots on its back. A swimming crab, it has two

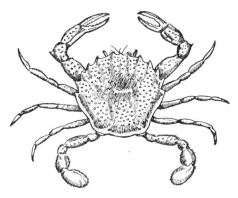

LADY CRAB

hind leg-paddles but it spends a great deal of time crawling along sandy bottoms. While sold by bait dealers, this crab can be caught by a manufactured crab net at low tide when visible. It has a habit if startled of burying itself in the sand with only the eyes protruding. If it is not visible, it can be caught by a home contrivance. Fasten a wire basket to the haft of a garden rake at a point where, when dislodged by the teeth of the rake, it will fall into it. Dislodging is accomplished by a quick twist of the rake handle when the crab is felt to be under the teeth.

The Lady Crab is also known as Calico Crab, Sand Crab and Speckled Crab. They are popular for Striped Bass bait.

FIDDLER CRABS

The Fiddler Crabs are distinguished from other Crabs by the unusual formation of the claws of the male. One claw is small, the other is large and out of proportion to its member claw.

Fiddlers inhabit sand and mud burrows in salt marshes and in brackish bays. They will live for several days after being

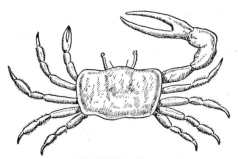

FIDDLER CRAB

caught in containers if they are not too crowded and the container is kept in a cool place.

Three species of Fiddler Crabs are found along the Atlantic shore from Florida to Cape Cod. The largest (*Uca minax*), also called Soldier Crab, is the red-jointed Fiddler. The red marks are on the joints of the large claw and the gray or brown color of its shell distinguishes it from the other Fiddlers. It prefers brackish or almost fresh water in marshes and here it digs holes above the high water mark.

Mud Fiddler (*Uca pugnax*)

One of the most numerous of the Crabs, the Mud Fiddler also called the Marsh Fiddler, is olive or dark green with yellowish claws. It prefers the mud flats of bays or inlets where it digs its burrows in the sedgy banks.

Sand Fiddler (*Uca pugilator*)

Also known as China-beak, the Sand Fiddler is somewhat smaller than the red-jointed Fiddler but larger than the Mud Fiddler. It is especially popular with fishermen for bait. It is somewhat light in color having a shiny, gray back with markings of dark gray, violet or brown. The claws are a pale yellow or of a white tinge. While it is often found living along with the Mud Fiddler, it usually prefers to dig its burrows in sandier soil.

Green Crab (*Carcinides maenas*)

While the Green Crab is considered a swimming crab it does not have hind legs shaped like paddles. In the main, it is a crawling crab and is common from Maine to New Jersey, being most plentiful in New England waters.

A small crab—two by three inches—it is a dark, drab green with yellow or yellowish-green spots. It is numerous in rocky

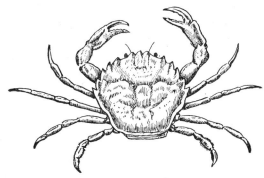

GREEN CRAB

areas, being found between low and high water marks in shallow pools where it hides under rocks, in crevices or in seaweed.

The Green Crab is hardy and will survive for days out of water if kept in a cool spot. They can also be kept alive in boxes submerged in water. Most bait shops sell this crab.

If the angler wishes to obtain the Green Crab in quantity, he should use a wire trap with two funnel entrances, similar somewhat to a minnow trap but with larger openings. Bait the trap with dead fish, crushed mussels or clams.

HERMIT CRABS (*Pagurus longicarpus*)

There are many species of the Hermit Crab along the Atlantic shore, some living in deep water, others in shallow. The most common of the Hermit Crabs is the *Pagurus longicarpus* which is only about an inch in length. It is generally found in the shells of small snails and periwinkles. It is abundant in the shallow waters and tidal pools from Florida to Massachusetts.

BIG HERMIT CRAB (*Pagurus pollicaris*)

This species lives in empty Whelk or Moon shells. Light brown or red, it is found in rocky and shell bottoms in bays and sounds from Maine to Florida.

Another species, *Pagurus bernhardus*, a larger red crab, ranges north from Cape Cod. It is found in deeper waters.

There are many other species of Hermit Crabs that are good for bait. When the Hermit Crab is used, it must first be

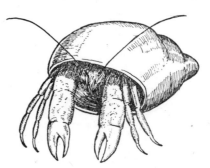

HERMIT CRAB

removed from the shell. This is done by cracking the shell with a hammer or rock. Heat applied will also bring the crab out into the open. Either the whole crab or the soft tail or belly can be placed on the hook as bait.

Crabs shed their shells at intervals as they attain various stages of growth, just as snakes shed their skins. During the period just prior to shedding their hard covering they are known as Shedder Crabs or Peelers. After the old shell is shed the Crab falls into the soft shell category. When it reaches the stage where the new shell is beginning to harden, but will still give under pressure, it is then called Paper-Back or Buckram. When the new shell becomes hard and rigid again, it has returned to the status of hard shell crab. While used for bait in all stages, the soft shell or shedder stage is usually preferred.

A shedder can be determined by trying to break off one of the movable pincers of the large claws. If it breaks with some difficulty leaving no meat exposed, it is a hard shell crab. Should it break easily, exposing newly-formed, soft meat, it is shedder crab.

SHRIMPS

Shrimps, in the main, look like small lobsters minus the two large claws. They have many tiny claws, a pair of long antennae and translucent or colorless, pink, pale green, green or blue bodies.

EDIBLE SHRIMP (*Peneus setiferus*)

The Edible Shrimp also called Common Shrimp, Southern Shrimp, Jumbo Shrimp and White Shrimp is the Shrimp found in restaurants, fish markets and bait shops. It averages about six inches but attains some ten inches in length. It is found from Virginia to the Gulf of Mexico. As an adult it generally

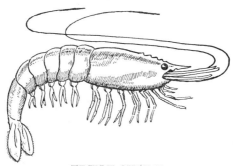

EDIBLE SHRIMP

seeks deep offshore waters; the younger ones frequent bays, inlets, sounds and rivers.

Two other relatives of the Edible Shrimp are also used extensively for bait. The Brazilian Shrimp (*Peneus braziliensis*) found from Florida to Cape Cod, and the Pink Shrimp (*Peneus duerarum*) which is confined mostly to the Gulf of Mexico.

The larger Shrimp are caught commercially, offshore; the smaller are taken close to shore in minnow seines or dip nets, netting them at night.

Shrimp are usually sold alive by bait dealers but, generally they are dead by the time the angler uses them for bait. To preserve dead Shrimp keep them on ice.

Common Sand Shrimp

Many species of this Shrimp are along the Atlantic coast in shallow water inlets, bays, sounds and in deeper offshore water. It hides in seaweed and among rocks but prefers to bury itself in sandy bottoms. Seldom exceeding three inches in length, it

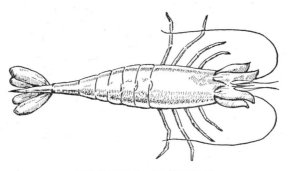

COMMON SAND SHRIMP

is a translucent, pale gray that is flecked with spots which vary in color in accordance to the bottom on which it happens to be lying.

The most numerous of the Sand Shrimps are the *Crago septemspinosus* and the *Crangon vulgaris,* found from Labrador to North Carolina. They are sold by bait dealers, but can also be caught with dip nets along rocky shores or in tidal pools. This Shrimp is an important bait.

Common Prawn (*Palaemonetes vulgaris*)

Also known as Grass Shrimp, Glass Prawn, Mud Shrimp, Harbor Shrimp, Pin Shrimp the Common Prawn is on the smallish side being generally about an inch and a half in length. But despite its small size, it is relished by many species of fish. Found in bays, estuaries, inlets and ditches, it ranges from Massachusetts to Florida. It is different from the Sand

Shrimp in that it has longer antennae and a pronounced sharp spine formation between the eyes. Its body, translucent and almost colorless, is spotted with brown.

The Common Prawn can easily be caught by anglers; it is just a simple matter of netting them with a small dip net of mesh wire or cloth. Look for them along the shore edge in

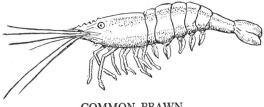

COMMON PRAWN

coves, mud flats and tidal creeks and hiding in eel grass. Once caught, put them in a bucket filled with sea water and keep it in a cool spot. Change the water frequently. However, if after catching them, the fisherman proceeds directly to his fishing, any wooden box will suffice with no water needed. Keep the box covered with a burlap sack and out of the sun or rain.

These small Shrimp are excellent for chumming, particularly for Weakfish. Throw them overboard, two or three at a time, at intervals.

Common Prawn

SAND BUGS (*Hippa talpoida*)

The Sand Bug, also called Beach Bug, Sand Crab, Mole Shrimp or Mole Crab, is easily identified by its egg shaped body with smooth back and stout and hairy legs protruding from the under side. It averages about an inch in length and is sometimes mistaken for the Sand Flea, which is smaller in size.

The smooth back of the Sand Bug is sand colored or tan, tinged with either a light purple or pink. It ranges from Florida to Cape Cod living on the open sandy beaches where it burrows under the breaking surf. On the incoming tide, it moves back up with it on the beach, then back down again to the low water mark as the tide goes out.

Sand Bugs live in colonies that number into the hundreds of thousands. Their presence can be detected by streaks in the sand caused by a prominence on the head that leaves a mark as the bug burrows backwards into the sand.

They can be dug up from under a breaking wave. Wait
until the water starts to recede then dig down into the wet
sand as far as possible and scoop up all the bugs the hands
encounter. To obtain them in quantity, use a dustpan-shaped
wire scoop of half-inch heavy mesh that is attached to a long
handle, the open end towards you. Wait until the wave breaks,

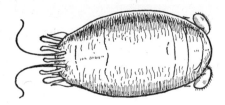

SAND BUG

then as its water recedes engage the sand with the scoop and
drag it towards you with its bottom lightly scraping the sand.
The half-inch mesh permits the sand and trash to pass through
but, except for the smaller bugs, you will trap a quantity of
Sand Bugs with each scoop.

The Sand Bug is good bait for the smaller species of fish.
If after larger fish, several of the bugs must be threaded on
the same hook in order to be effective.

The fisherman can keep a supply on hand for a considerable
time if they are kept in a sand box.

BAIT-FISH

The many species of fish that are used for bait and are
designated as "bait-fish", range from two inches to two or
more feet in length. They travel in schools numbering into the
hundreds of thousands and are found in bays, inlets, rivers,
the surf and miles off-shore.

MENHADEN   Average Length: 4 to
(Brevoortia tyrannus)   12 in.
Family: Herring (*Clupeidae*)
Also known as: Bunker, Fat-back,
Pogy, Bugfish, Hardhead, etc.

The Menhaden is a flat, deep-bodied fish with a broad back
and slim belly. Its upper half is a blueish color blending into

silvery sides which sometime have a brassy tinge. The adult has a large dark spot just back of the gill opening on the shoulder and smaller spots along the upper sides.

An oily fish when ground up, it is most admirable for chum, as the natural oils attract fish from afar. The larger Menhaden (some reach 18 inches in length) is used for large game fish.

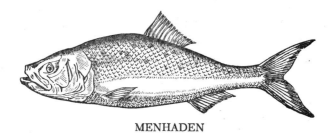

MENHADEN

It can, however, be cut into strips of any desired length for smaller fish. The smaller Menhaden is used intact for the smaller species of fish.

Schools of Menhaden, being very compact, cause a distinctive ripple in the water by which the school can be spotted.

Most bait dealers sell them.

STRIPED MULLET   Average Length: 3 to
(Mugil cephalus)   12 in.
Family: *Muglidae*
Also known as Common Mullet and
Jumping Mullet.

The Striped Mullet has a dark blue back with noticeable stripes and silvery sides. It travels in schools of thousands, swimming along the coast, the passage of the school being marked by the dark patch on the water that their compactness creates. An easily frightened fish, it leaps from the water at the slightest provocation, and especially when being chased by game fish.

Mullet are found in inlets, bays, sounds and rivers, feeding over both mud and sandy bottoms.

A close relative, the White Mullet (*Mugil curema*) also known as the Silver Mullet, is similar in appearance to the Striped Mullet with the exception that it lacks the stripes and the back is more olive green in color. It reaches three feet in length as the extreme, a foot longer than the Striped Mullet.

The Mullet can be used whole for big fish or cut into strips or chunks of different sizes for bottom fishing. Generally the

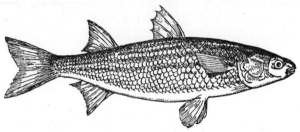

STRIPED MULLET

fish is scaled before cutting to prevent any of the tough scales lodging on the point of the hook.

Fish markets, commercial fishermen and most bait shops sell them.

ATLANTIC HERRING   AVERAGE LENGTH: 9 to
(Clupea harengus)   12 in.
Family: *Clupeidae*
Also called: Common Herring, Sea
Herring and Labrador Herring.

The Atlantic Herring is a thin fish with a greenish or blueish back and silvery sides. It is a member of one of the most numerous families of fishes in the North Atlantic Ocean, mil-

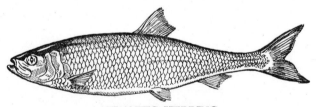

ATLANTIC HERRING

lions of pounds being taken annually. The Herring swim in large schools and are caught commercially in seines, weirs, traps and nets. It is a difficult fish for the angler to keep alive for any length of time. Herring is generally purchased from seiners and commercial trollers.

ALEWIFE   AVERAGE LENGTH: 12 in.
(Polomolobus pseudo-harengus)
Family: *Clupeidae*
Also called Branch Herring, Buckie,
Spring Herring, Sawbelly, Grayback,
etc.

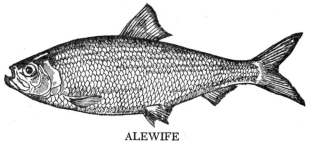

ALEWIFE

This member of the Herring family somewhat resembles the
Shad in appearance. It is caught in large numbers by commercial fishermen and is an excellent bait for the many species
of fish that feed on the Herring family. It is sold mainly by
commercial boats.

GLUT HERRING   AVERAGE LENGTH: 8 to
(Pomolobus aestivalis)   12 in.
Family: *Clupeidae*
Also called: Summer Herring, Blue-
back, Kyack and Blackbelly.

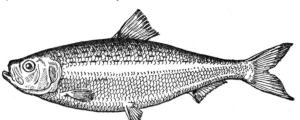

GLUT HERRING

This fish is a close relative of the Alewife and is most abundant in Chesapeake Bay. It ascends salt streams to spawn. It is
caught in the same manner as other species of Herring and is
sold by commercial boats.

HICKORY SHAD   AVERAGE LENGTH: 20 to
(Pomolobus mediocris)   24 in.
Family: *Clupeidae*
Also called: Shad Herring, Tailor
Herring and Fall Herring.

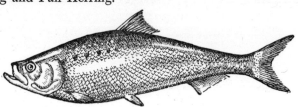

HICKORY SHAD

This is another species of bait fish that resembles the Alewife
and the Shad. It reaches a greater length and weight than the
Alewife, but does not attain the size of the Shad. It is of a size
that can readily be caught with rod and reel and the smaller
ones can be used whole for certain species of fish. The larger
ones can be cut into strips for other species. It is sold by commercial boats.

KILLIFISH, COMMON   AVERAGE LENGTH: 3 to
(Fundulus heteroclitus)   5 in.
Family: *Fundulus*
Also called: Mud Dabber, Mummy,
Hardhead, Mud Minnow, Common
Mummichog.

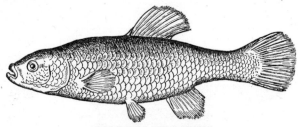

COMMON KILLIFISH

There are many species of the Killifish but the one most
favored for bait is the Common Killifish. It is easily recognized
by the single dorsal fin set well back towards its blunted tail.
It has a heavily scaled body that is olive-green, with yellowish
or whitish belly, all on the drab side. Some of the Common

Killifish have spots or vertical narrow bars along the sides. This fish is generally found in large schools in salt water bays, inlets, tidal creeks and rivers; where ever there are plenty of weeds. They are readily caught with seines or minnow traps and nets. A hardy fish, it lives for a considerable time on the hook, or if kept out of water. They also survive in fresh water which is not a trait of other salt water fish.

Bait dealers carry this baitfish when the Summer Flounder, or Fluke, is running and it can also be obtained later in the season, during the winter, for ice fishing.

STRIPED KILLIFISH   Average Length: 4 in.
(Fundulus majalis)
Family: *Fundulus*
Also called: Striped Mummichog, Mummy and Striped Killie.

STRIPED KILLIFISH

Another species of the Killifish that is used occasionally for bait is the Striped Killifish. It is found in the same waters as the Common Killifish. It differs somewhat in appearance being lighter in color and having a longer, more slender body with dark, vertical stripes on its sides. These stripes sometimes cause it to be mistaken for a young Striped Bass. Its dorsal fin is set about the same as that of the Common Killifish but its tail is less blunt.

Bait dealers sell the Striped Killifish, mixed with other small bait fish as a rule.

BROAD KILLIFISH   Average Length: 2 to
(Cyprinodon variegatus)   3 in.
Family: *Fundulus*
Also called Sheepshead Minnow.

This third member of the family is also used for bait. It is similar to the Common Killifish with the exception that its body is broader, hence the name. Found in the same waters as the Common and Striped Killifish, it is sold, mixed with other small baitfish, by bait dealers.

SILVERSIDES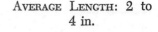
(Menidia menidia)
Family: *Atheridae*
Also called Shiner, sand Bait, Sperling and White Bait.

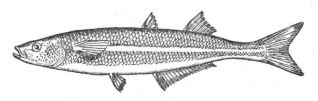

SILVERSIDES

Many species of Silversides abound along the Atlantic coast, furnishing food for many species of fish. In color, the Silversides has a pale green body with silvery bands running along the sides. This fish is found practically the year round in bays, rivers and the surf, being most numerous in late summer, fall and early winter. They are caught in Seines, minnow nets or drop nets. A delicate fish, they die quickly in confinement or on the hook, but it is an excellent bait, dead or alive. Silversides are sold by most bait dealers.

SAND LAUNCE   AVERAGE LENGTH: 10 in.
(Ammodytes americanus)
Family: *Ammodytes*
Also called Sand Eel.

SAND LAUNCE

This fish is very similar in appearance to the Eel but it possesses a forked tail which the Eel does not. Not as widely known as other baitfish, it is, nevertheless, an excellent bait.

It is blueish in color with a white belly and swims in schools in both deep and shallow water. It likes sandy bottoms and will bury itself to a depth of some five inches in the sand.

The Sand Launce is a tough bait that remains on the hook for a considerable time. The smaller ones are used whole; the larger are cut into halves for the smaller fishes. Particularly abundant in the late fall, the Sand Launce is sold by most bait dealers.

ATLANTIC MACKEREL   Average Length: 12 to
(Scomber scombrus)   15 in.
Family: *Scombridae*
Also called Common Mackerel.

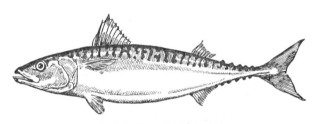

ATLANTIC MACKEREL

This fish is identified by its streamlined body, blue or greenish in color, with dark bars spaced along the back. It is very popular as bait, the larger Mackerel being used by sport fishermen for the large game fish, the smaller for smaller game fish such as Bluefish, Striped Bass and Codfish. The Mackerel migrates seasonly in great schools. It is sold by bait dealers and fish markets.

COMMON EEL   Average Length: 6 in.
(Anguilla rostrata)   to 2 ft.
Family: *Apodes*
Also called Fresh-water Eel and
American Eel.

The Eel, a favorite bait for many salt water fishermen, is most numerous in bays, sounds, tidal creeks, rivers and fresh water lakes. Shaped like a snake, its body varies in color being olive, gray, brown, blackish along the back with a white, yellow or silver belly. The females are the larger, reaching some four feet in length; the males are seldom more than two feet. Both are good for bait but the preference is the smaller male, usually caught in brackish waters.

The most dependable method for catching Eels is the eel pot, which is set out at night, baited with dead fish, mussels, clams or crabs. The eel pot is made of wood or metal frames with wire mesh and is shaped, somewhat, like a minnow trap.

COMMON EEL

Eels are also taken with rod and reel, seines and several-pronged fish spears.

Eels are a hardy fish, but, due to the difficulty in handling them, they are generally killed before using them for bait. They can be used whole—seven to twenty inches in length—or cut into pieces or sections. If fishing for Striped Bass, it is best to have the Eel alive.

The skin of the Eel is also used on various metal squids or Eelskin lures.

CHAPTER VI

Methods

BAITFISH

Through the lips, barb down, for Trolling.

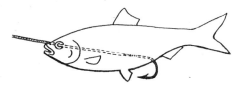

Through both eyes and the stomach. Trolling and casting.

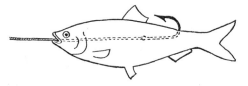

Through the back for Float fishing and casting.

There are other methods of hooking bait-fish but I recommend these three as being the most satisfactory.

SHRIMP

Two small Shrimp on one
hook. Heads are in reverse.

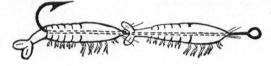

Peeled tail of large Shrimp.

Sand Shrimp h o o k e d
through the back near the tail.
Barb is under the Shrimp.

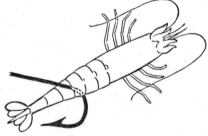

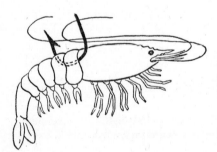

Edible Shrimp h o o k e d
through the back towards the
head. Barb on top of the
Shrimp.

CLAMS

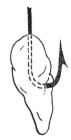

A small piece of Clam baited for small fish.

The whole Clam baited for large fish.

CRABS

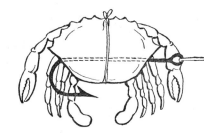

Soft Shell Crab. Hook through practically at the center and tie with light thread. Dead.

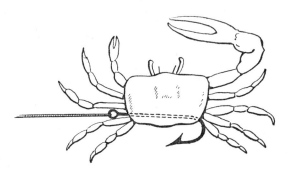

A Fiddler Crab, hooked through the base near the edge. The Crab is alive.

One half of a Green Crab
hooked through base near the
edge.

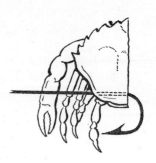

. The Blue Crab, Lady Crab
and all other Hard Shell Crabs
are hooked in the same manner as the Fiddler Crab.

All Soft Shell Crabs are
hooked and tied as is the Soft
Shell Crab that is illustrated.

MUSSEL
Thread on and tie with
thread at curve of the barb.

WHELK, CONCH
Hooked on from curve of
shank half way up shank.

SQUID

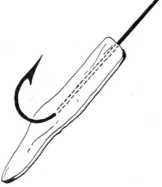

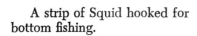
A strip of Squid hooked for bottom fishing.

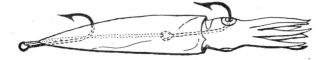

Whole Squid hooked for bottom fishing.

Head of Squid hooked for bottom fishing.

SAND BUG
Hook through back.

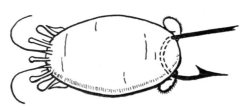

SNAIL

Soft part dangles.

WORMS

Blood Worm. Hook through skin, not body. Tail must dangle.

Sand Worm. Head at curve of shank. Tail must dangle.

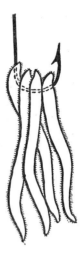

Sand or Blood Worms, several on a hook. Tails must hang straight from curve of shank.

Small portion of worm for small fish. Tail must dangle.

Single worm threaded up the shank of the hook. Tail must dangle.

PLUGS AND METAL SQUIDS

PLUGS

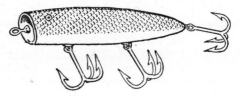

"Popping" Surface Plug

The nose is hollow to a depth of about ¼ inch. When the rod is jerked—every few turns of the reel—water pops in and out of this hollow, making a commotion, a popping sound on the surface.

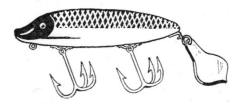

"FlaP-Tail" Surface Plug

As the plug is reeled in, a spinner-like tail revolves making a commotion on the surface.

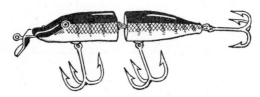

Jointed Under-Water Plug

Due to its construction, this plug goes deep in the water and the jointed section wiggles, resembling a fish swimming.

Diving "Wobbler" Plug

Due to its construction, the plug rides deep and the whole plug wiggles, making a commotion under the surface.

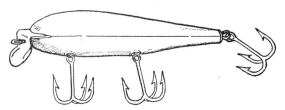

Large Surface Plug

This plug, designed for large fish, rides the surface. It can also be used for an Eelskin rig.

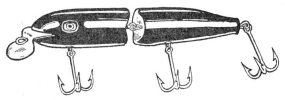

Large Under-Water Jointed Plug

When in the water, this plug looks and acts like a swimming eel.

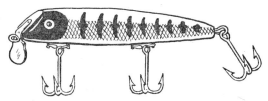

Small Surface Plug

This plug is used with a light rod or a Spinning rod. It rides the surface.

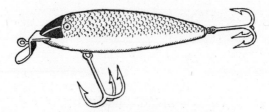

Under-Water Mullet-Type Plug
It somewhat resembles the Mullet in the water.

METAL SQUIDS

Large Mullet Squid

Diamond Squid

Sand Eel Squid With Tail Hook and Pork Rind

Small Sand Eel Squid

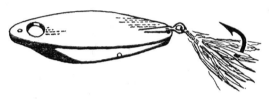

Narragansett Rowboat Squid

Silversides Squid

SINKERS AND SWIVELS

Sinkers

Bank Sinker
This sinker is used on rocky bottoms where, due to its shape, it can slide between rocks and through crevices.

Pyramid Sinker
Used on sandy bottoms, this sinker digs into sand and holds fast against normal water action.

Clincher Sinker
Pinched onto a line, this sinker adds weight to take the bait or lure deeper down. It can easily be removed.

Ball Sinker
The Ball Sinker rolls along until it stops in a sand hole or against a rock where fish are generally feeding.

Swivels

Three Way Swivel

This Swivel has the fishline fastened to one eye, the sinker to a second and the leader with bait or lure to the third. It keeps the three from tangling in the water.

Barrel (Two Way) Swivel

One eye of the Swivel is used to fasten to the fishing line, the other to a leader, sinker or leader hook.

Connecting Link

This device connects the line and leader or line and rig. It opens at either end thus permitting a change without cutting the line.

FISH FINDER

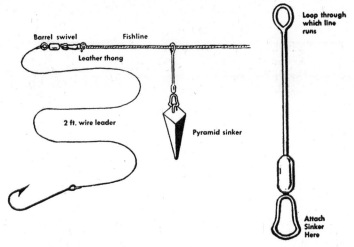

The fishline passes through the rigid upper eye and the sinker is fastened to the lower, non-rigid eye. The sinker anchors in the sand and the line and leader play about freely through the rigid eye above it, "finding fish." The line cannot back up through the eye due to the leather thong being larger than the eye.

SPREADER

This device attached to a fishline has an eye at each end to which leader and hook are attached. It keeps the hooks apart when in the water.

DRAIL AND CLOTHES PIN

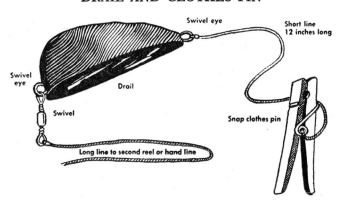

Swivel eye

Short line
12 inches long

Swivel
eye

Drail

Swivel

Snap clothes pin

Long line to second reel or hand line

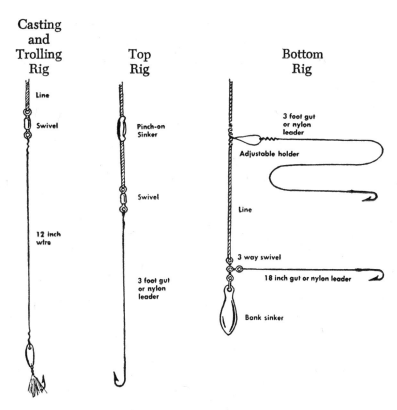

**Casting
and
Trolling
Rig**

Line

Swivel

12 inch
wire

**Top
Rig**

Pinch-on
Sinker

Swivel

3 foot gut
or nylon
leader

**Bottom
Rig**

3 foot gut
or nylon
leader

Adjustable holder

Line

3 way swivel

18 inch gut or nylon leader

Bank sinker

Deep Sea Rig

Float Rig Casting

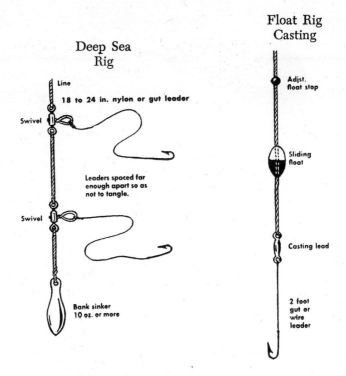

Line

18 to 24 in. nylon or gut leader

Swivel

Leaders spaced far enough apart so as not to tangle.

Swivel

Bank sinker 10 oz. or more

Adjst. float stop

Sliding float

Casting lead

2 foot gut or wire leader

Hook Arm on Bottom Rig Leader

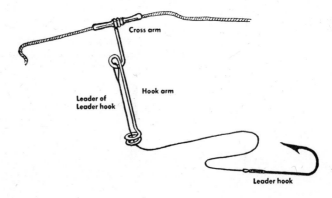

Cross arm

Leader of Leader hook

Hook arm

Leader hook

ROD WINDING and FISHERMEN'S KNOTS

Rod Winding

The trick to rod winding lies in the beginning and the end. Use a size A silk thread or a size D. Size A is rather fine and gives a neater appearing job; size D is heavier and easier to wind.

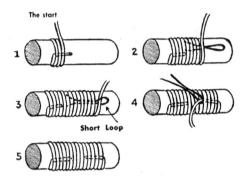

1. Tuck the end of the thread under the first three or four windings.

2. Then continue winding until the end of the tucked under thread is covered by four or five turns.

3. Take a short, separate piece of thread and loop it. Place this piece of looped thread on the windings, the loop faced out and beyond the last turn. Wind until the loop is narrowed to the point where the winding line can just be threaded through it.

4. Grasp the protruding ends of the buried loop and pull; the winding thread will come out back, and underneath the last several turns.

5. With a razor blade cut the winding thread close to the windings and the result will be an invisible "knot."

FISHERMEN'S KNOTS

Twist Knot. For tying the line to a swivel.

Twist Knot. For tying a gut leader. Leader must be well soaked first.

Turtle Knot. For tying on eyed hooks.

Loop. Tie each knot ¼ in. apart. Tighten each knot before tying the next one. Tie six knots or more.

Barrel Knot. After completing loops, pull both ends tight. This is the simplest knot that will not slip on or cut nylon line.

Calcutta or Burma Cane-stick Rod

Should the angler wish to make an inexpensive rod, he should by a very light Calcutta or Burma cane-stick 13 to 16 feet in length. The cane-stick comes heavier and thicker at one end than the other. From the top—the lightest section—cut off between 1 to 3 feet depending on how long a rod is desired. Then, by means of the reel clamps, attach the reel to the bottom section 24 to 30 inches from the end. Next the guides—the metal loops through which the line runs from the reel along the rod. First comes the tip-top guide which is fitted to the end of the top, cemented in place with special ferrule cement. Then by means of Scotch tape, align the guides with the reel and secure them, spaced at regular intervals from the tip-top guide down to reel. The guides are secured by their arms, and the intervals vary according to the number of guides used and the length of the rod. From 3 to 5 guides are recommended. The guides vary in diameter; the smallest is placed next after the tip-top guide then graduate down to the largest guide.

To give an example. The original cane-stick is say, 14 feet long. Two feet are cut from the top leaving a rod 12 feet in length. Secure the tip-top guide; secure the reel, setting it 24 inches from the end of the rod. Three guides are to be used besides the top guide. These should be spaced at even intervals of 30 inches from the top guide to the reel. Be sure to set the guides squarely in line with the reel.

To wind the guides firmly on the reel, after setting them with Scotch tape, use a D or EE silk thread. The winding on of the guides is the same process as rod winding (page 185). The winding can be started at any distance from the end of the guide arm to dress up the rod. But if no extra winding is desired, start winding on the rod one-quarter of an inch from the end of the guide arm. Wind towards the base of the guide. Insert the end of the thread under the first three turns; then wind onto the guide arm to within a half-inch of the base of the guide. Here, insert the extra piece of looped thread—as in rod winding— then continue the turns to practically the base of the guide. Pass the end of the winding thread through the loop; then pull both of the loose ends of the extra piece of looped thread. The winding line will come out under the windings. Cut off close with a razor blade. Repeat this process on the other arm of the guide.

To preserve the color of the winding thread, apply Color Preservative, a liquid, with a small brush or the finger. After it dries varnish the windings with a rod varnish.

A LARGE GUIDE

GUIDE WINDING

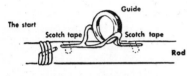

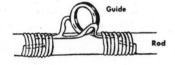

TIP-TOP GUIDE

Home Made Wooden Plug

The easiest method is to use a lathe, but if the angler does not own or have access to one, the plug can be fashioned by hand. Obtain a small block of maple or red cedar, and with a sharp knife and file, shape the block into a form that resembles a fish. Then with a very small drill, drill a hole the length of

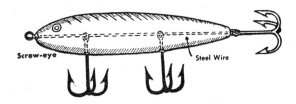

the plug being careful to keep it centered. Run a length of steel wire through this hole to protrude from both ends. On one end of the wire fasten a screw-eye, on the other a treble hook. Then drill two holes in the belly of the plug deep enough so that two bottom hooks can be attached to the central wire. Give the plug at least two coats of paint, any color desired, and then finish off with a coat of clear varnish.

Sylvester Wood Float

From a hardware store obtain a dowel or two. With knife and file, form the dowel into a top-like shape that is about 5 inches long and tapers from a top of from 1½ to 2 inches to a bottom about an inch wide. Insert a screw-eye in each end; fasten to the upper screw-eye a wire leader 18 to 24 inches long, with feathers.

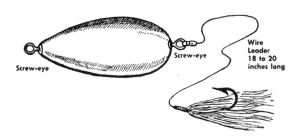

TACKLE CARE

Salt water is hard on tackle, for salt rusts and corrodes metal, and sand and rocks fray and wear lines. Bamboo rods are quickly ruined if the salt water penetrates the sections that have been glued together. Just as it is advisable to clean a gun shortly after it has been fired, so should the angler acquire the habit of caring for his tackle soon after its use. It will pay him to do so in the long run.

DRYING THE LINE

Linen lines should be cared for as soon as possible after being immersed in salt water. The longer the line remains with salt on it, the weaker it becomes. The best method for drying is to use a line dryer. This is a devise made of wood and is shaped like a spool that is mounted horizontally on a stand. There is a handle for turning the spool to play the line off of the reel and onto it.

If there is no spool dryer available, the fisherman can tie the end of the line to a tree limb, post or large nail in a building and then walk to an adoining tree, post or nail, engage the line thereon and walk back to repeat this process until the line has paid off the reel. The line should then remain suspended until dry. Do not, however, dry out a line in full sunlight.

Another method is to first rinse the line off thoroughly in fresh water and then wrap it evenly around a folded newspaper and leave until dry.

Nylon lines require less care than linen lines, since nylon does not readily absorb water. But, since there is always some moisture present on the line after fishing, it is a sensible practice to dry it but not necessary.

The monafillament lines used in spinning do not require drying; they do not absorb or retain moisture.

ROD, REEL AND METAL PARTS

The whole rod should be varnished at the beginning of each fishing season. This prevents the silk thread on rod and guides from unravelling when they become wet after some months of being out of the water.

The reel should be oiled and greased each time before going out to fish. Well cared for in this manner the salt in the water cannot clog nor freeze the mechanism of the reel. A properly lubricated reel is a long-life reel, so it pays to take this trouble.

Ferrules, guides and other metal parts of the equipment, such as the steel spring on a tilt, can be cleaned and preserved with nickle polish.

When not in use, hang the rods up by means of the tip top guide, preferably in a cool place.

When putting a reel away for some time, oil all its parts. It is not necessary to take the reel apart if the oiling is done properly.

Before going out with a glass rod that has been inactive for some time, check the ferrule; the cement may have dried out and it will be loose. In this case, heat and add a little more cement to make it firm.

After fishing, wipe a beryllium rod clean with a cloth. Glass rods do not need to be wiped.

CHAPTER VII

※

The Fisherman's Principles

When going to a tackle shop to invest in fishing equipment take an experienced friend along with you if possible.

❖ ❖

If such a friend cannot accompany you, do not buy the first article that is shown you by the clerk or shop owner. Shop a bit, ask questions and have him explain everything to your satisfaction.

❖ ❖

However, if you know him to be a real fisherman, abide by his suggestions. He will be able to outfit you with the proper tackle based on your age, occupation and weight.

❖ ❖

Fishing can be tiresome if the wrong tackle is used.

❖ ❖

A big, husky man can use either light or heavy tackle; a shorty of one hundred and forty pounds should use light tackle; heavy equipment will tire him out in a short time when casting.

❖ ❖

Bait and tackle shop owners appreciate a purchase no matter how small. It is not mandatory, but if seeking information, make a small purchase of some kind. You'll get the information, regardless, and your consideration promotes good will.

❖ ❖

When going fishing, always take some extra clothes with you. The city may be hot, but on or near the water it is generally quite chilly, and you may get wet.

❖ ❖

Good fishing depends to a great extent on winds and tides. Learn to know the speed of the tide.

More experimentation is required with lures, baits, tackle and methods of retrieving in the early spring than is necessary in the later fishing seasons.

          ❖   ❖

A good fisherman catches fish, when they are biting, because of his know-how in regards to bait, lure and fishing technique. A poor fisherman, or a beginner, will not get fish due to lack of knowledge.

          ❖   ❖

Nature's fishing secrets are well protected; it is not easy to solve them. But knowledge is gained through trial, error, willingness to accept qualified advice, and observation.

          ❖   ❖

The rank of top flight fisherman is obtained by patience; determination; perseverence; the use of the correct tackle and,- observation.

          ❖   ❖

Observe and learn the habits of fish.

          ❖   ❖

Observe and remember water conditions at the time you catch fish. Was it rough; choppy; smooth; cold; warm; clear; roiled?

          ❖   ❖

Observe the action of the tide and undertow if any.

          ❖   ❖

Observe, if fishing at night, the phase of the moon. Full; new; what quarter? Each phase of the moon affects the feeding of the fish.

          ❖   ❖

Observe the sky, particularly if in a rowboat. A Mackerel sky generally means rain the next day; mountainous white clouds may indicate the approach of a northwester, a heavy rain and windstorm that breaks quickly.

          ❖   ❖

A cloudless sky generally means no strong wind that day.

          ❖   ❖

Dark, fast-moving clouds bring a fast wind within a few hours.

          ❖   ❖

A hanging mist means there will be little wind while it prevails.

CASTING

When learning to cast, do not handicap yourself by starting out forming bad habits. These habits will have to be overcome later.

❀ ❀

When starting to learn to cast, begin casting *very easily.* Use the hands and wrists, *not* the arms and shoulders. The hand and wrist action plus the whip of the rod are sufficient to send out the lure.

❀ ❀

The right handed surf caster grips the butt of the rod with his right hand and gives the snap with his left hand and wrist; the left hander does just the reverse.

❀ ❀

Using easy wrist action, learn the "feel" of the rod. Once this "feel" is mastered, the power of the wrist-snap can be increased.

❀ ❀

Easy does it. The golfer presses and loses control. The caster, beginner or veteran, tries to "powerhouse his cast." Result: poor control and poor casting.

❀ ❀

Remember that when the forward motion of the rod tip reaches about eleven o'clock, the forward motion should cease, as the line is released.

❀ ❀

On a still day the average surf fishing cast is about 150 feet. The wind against the caster, the average cast is about 120 feet. The wind behind the caster, the average cast is about 160 to 175 feet.

❀ ❀

Unless casting with a plug, the wind does not retard the cast to any great extent. Many fishermen, facing a wind, feel more power must be used, and this often results in a backlash.

❀ ❀

Relax and cast as usual; there will be but a few feet variance in the distance of the cast.

❀ ❀

FISHING

Don't, when a fish strikes, set the hook with a jerk. A quick, steady pull is all that is necessary to imbed the hook.

Don't leave a rod in gear when it is in a sand spike and the baited hook is in the water. In gear, a large fish can take rod, reel and line out to sea before the fisherman can prevent it.

* *

Always put the rod into free spool with the ratchet on. The ratchet will click the signal when a fish has taken the bait.

* *

Never lay the reel down on the sand. The sand can get into the mechanism, even though well-oiled, and spoil the days fishing.

* *

Always be provided with plenty of bait so as to ensure not running short before the day's fishing is over.

* *

Always have a pair of small cutting pliers in your kit. Should a hook become imbedded in a hand or finger, cut off the eye-end of the hook and then *push the hook through the flesh* and out.

* *

Never try to *pull* the hook out; its barb makes this either impossible, or this operation will badly lacerate the hand or finger.

* *

Never rush to grab hold of a landed fish. Twisting and flaping about, there is always the chance of a hook snagging the over-anxious angler.

* * *

TOURNAMENT CASTING

Just prior to World War II a group of men pioneered in forming a Tournament Casting Association. Fred Evers, Belmar, N. J.; Robert Linten, Jamestown, R. I.; Joe Chapdalane, Wickford, R. I.; Otto Lang, New York; Ned Nardin, New York; Honk Clark, Narragansett, R. I.; Nick Guarino, Belmar, N. J.; Davis of Taunton, Mass.; the Bowman Brothers, Philadelphia and several others whose names escape me.

New York officials cooperating, we held our meets along the beaches of Coney Island and at the Jamaica race track during the off season. We met on Sundays, holidays and in the evenings, and, forming three- to five-man teams, we competed, casting for distance and accuracy. Our Association received national recognition.

These men, all veteran fishermen, were in full accord with me in the idea of promoting a Tournament Casting along the lines of the present day Little League Baseball Clubs. While all ages would be welcome, we particularly wanted the teen-agers and younger children to become interested and form clubs.

The War put a crimp in our operations and our idea, but it is to be hoped that it will be taken up again and local clubs formed, not only in these parts, but throughout the country, stressing teen-age participation.

A great deal can be learned in regards to handling rod and reel from Tournament Casting. It is also a healthy sport that gets one out into the fresh air, teaches good sportsmanship and encourages potential fishermen. Those who indulge will soon want to try their new-found skill along the beaches.

Tournament Casting is so competitive that, in the case of us older men, we were often in a tizzy trying to decide, on any given day, whether to hold a meet or go fishing. It is great fun.

A FINAL WORD

To the new fisherman:

Never forget in your enthusiasm, that the other fellow has his rights too.

Do not crowd around a successful angler or try to fish his particular spot because he is catching fish.

If an angler close by has a fish on and is playing him, reel in so as not to have your line tangle with his. Give him every opportunity to land his fish.

If forced to wait for a change of tide, do not fuss and fret, being a sour-puss. Relax and exchange information and fishing experiences; you can always learn from the other fellow. Relax and enjoy the beauties of Nature around you. Cussin' and fussin' won't hurry up matters one little bit.

Do not trespass and do not damage property. Be a good sport and you will find that fishing is fun . . . Fishing is easy.

APPENDIX A

※

Preparing Fish

To FILLET:

Place the fish on a board or flat surface and, with a sharp knife, slit the side of the fish's head down from the dorsal (back) fin to under the throat. Repeat the operation on the other side so that the two cuts crisscross under the throat. Do *not* sever the head completely; it serves as a means of holding the fish in place.

Next, slit open the belly from the crisscross of the throat incision to the tail and remove the insides. Open the fish; laying it flat on the board and with a sharp knife blade gently slice the meat from off the backbone and the boney structure. Lift the meat intact.

To SKIN:

Cut around the head as described in the operation to fillet. Then pry up a small section of the fish's skin just below the incision; hold the fish firmly down by the head, and with a pair of pliers pull the skin down to the tail. Cut off the skin and tail.

To REMOVE SCALES:

Hold the fish flat by the head on a board. Use the blade of a fish knife or fish scaler. Hold the blade at right angles to the fish's body and move it back and forth in a scrubbing motion, exerting whatever pressure is needed to remove the scales.

Pollack, Weakfish, Bluefish and Cod should be cleaned as soon as possible. Do not leave them uncleaned overnight.

Striped Bass are an exception; they can be kept longer intact than if cleaned.

APPENDIX B

Glossary For Beginners

BACKLASH. A snarled tangle of the fishing line that is on the spool of the reel which is caused by the spool revolving at a speed that is faster than that of the line paying off the spool on the cast.

BLOCKTIN JIG. A fish-shaped piece of tin having either a swinging or stationary hook attached to one end. The opposite end has a hole in which to fasten the leader.

BOTTOM FISHING. The fishing line is let down into the water until the sinker on the end of the line rests on the bottom.

BUCKTAIL. An artificial lure made of hairs taken from the tail of a buck deer. These hairs are tied over a fishhook and the lure resembles a fish when in the water.

CHUM OR TO CHUM. Chum is ground-up fish: mussels; clams; crabs, etc. The preparation is either thrown into the water, a handfull at a time, or placed in the water in a bag. It attracts the fish as the natural oils seep from the bag to form a stream or slick. To CHUM is the act of putting Chum into the water.

DISGORGER. A metal rod so fashioned at one end that a deeply swallowed hook can be engaged and extracted from the stomach of the fish.

DRAG. A mechanical brake that is built into a reel and which can be applied to slow down the speed of the line as it leaves the reel spool.

DRAIL. A piece of half-moon-shaped metal weighing from ½ to 5 pounds having a swivel at either end. At one end, the long line of a *second* fishing rod is attached; at the other, a short line of 12 inches. To this short line is fastened a snap clothes pin.

Two rods are used when a drail is employed, the fishing rod proper and the second or drail rod. The purpose of the drail is to hold the lure on the fishing rod at any desired depth. To illustrate: the angler wishes to fish at say, 25 feet depth. First 25 feet is measured off on the drail line on the second rod and the line secured. Then the clothes pin is clipped on the fishing line from 5 to 15 inches above the lure. When both lines go into the water, simultaneously, the drail line pays out 25 feet, and stops, holding the lure at that depth. When a fish strikes the lure, the line comes free from the clothes pin thus relieving the angler of the extra weight that served to carry the lure down—something to be considered during a long fight with a big fish.

FEATHERS. An artificial lure made of the hackle feathers of a fowl or of a buck deer's tail hairs combined with nylon and tied onto or over a fish hook.

FERRULE. The ferrule is made of plated brass and comes in two parts, "male" and "female." The male section fits on the butt end of the rod tip; the female section fits on the upper, small end of the rod butt. The male section fits into the female section, thus forming the rod proper. There is an area on the female section which is the rod seat. On this is placed the reel,

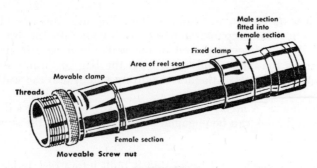

FERRULE

one arm fitting into a fixed clamp at the upper end of the area, the other arm fitting into a movable clamp at the lower end of the area. The reel in place, it is secured by means of a round, movable screw nut which is advanced to engage the lower clamp on the lower reel arm, firm. This nut, in turn, is secured by threads on the ferrule.

FISH FINDER. The Fish Finder is comprised of: a short metal bar with an eye in either end, a short leather thong, a pyramid sinker snapped on to the end of a length of metal that is about 8 inches long and which has an eye on the other end. The fishline is passed through this eye and then is attached to the leather thong which, in turn, is fastened to one of the eyes of the bar. The leader is attached to the other eye of the bar.

The sinker drops to the bottom and holds fast while the line plays free through the bar eye, (about 8 inches above the sinker) and is carried hither and yon by the action of the water. The line cannot back up through the eye because the thong is larger than the eye of the metal length from which the pyramid sinker dangles. Thus the hook cannot tangle with the line as it floats about. *See illustration page 182.*

FLOAT. A piece of wood, plastic or cork, generally round or oval in shape which is fastened to the fishline. It floats on the surface of the water, holding the bait at any desired distance below it.

FLOAT FISHING. Fishing with a float made of wood, cork or plastic, that is attached to the line. The float, bobbing along on the surface, keeps the bait suspended at the desired distance in the water beneath it.

FOUL HOOKED. This term is used when a fish is accidentally caught by a hook that is imbedded in its tail, back, side or stomach.

FREE LINE. Fishing with a line which has only a lure on it— no sinker whose weight would carry the lure down in the water.

FREE SPOOL. Fishing with a line that has no drag (brake) set on the reel, as the line leaves the reel spool.

GAFF. A barbless over-sized hook attached to the end of a

length of metal or wood about 2 to 10 feet long. It is used to reach down to hook the gills of a fish that has been caught and lift it from the water.

Guide. A metal circle of varying sizes that has two arms. They are fastened to the fishing rod at spaced intervals by means of a strong thread which binds the arms to the rod. One guide, the tip top guide, is always at the tip of the rod. The line runs through these guides from the reel.

Hook Arm. Made of metal, two coiled rings form one end from which the shank extends about 1½ inches to a single ring and then on for about ¾ inch to a hollow cross bar. This cross bar, about 1 inch long, is clipped on to a wire or nylon leader used as a bottom rig. Generally two hook arms are used. The leader of the leader hook is secured by the single hook arm ring and then passed down along the shank of the hook arm and through the two coiled rings at the end. The whole contrivance is similar to a spreader in that it keeps the hooks from tangling with the line when in the water. *See illustration page 184.*

Hook Shank. The body of the fishhook. It has a sharp-pointed barb at one end and an eye in the other end. The leader is attached to the hook by means of this eye; the barb holds the bait and also serves to penetrate the membrane of the mouth of the fish.

Inshore. Fishing in waters that are relatively close to shore, or just off the shore, as opposed to the open sea.

Jig. A piece of shiny, fish-shaped metal of from ½ to 5 ounces in weight. It has a fish hook attached to one end. Or it is a fish hook partially hidden in feathers. The opposite end has an eye in which the leader is attached.

Leader. A varying length of nylon, gut, stainless steel cable or piano wire. One end fastens to the lure or the hook; the other end fastens to the line. It protects the line from friction against rocks and rocky ledges, water action, and the abrasion of sand. It also protects against the teeth of certain species of fish.

Live Line. Another term for Free Line fishing.

LURE. Any artificial bait, such as a plug, spoon, spinner or feathered jig.

METAL SQUID. A fish-shaped lure made from all kinds of metal. It can have a single fixed hook at one end or, a fixed hook and swinging hook. The other end has an eye in which the leader is attached.

OFFSHORE. Fishing in waters in the open ocean.

PLUG. An artificial lure made of plastic or wood that resembles a fish in shape and coloring. It has from one to three hooks attached to it, generally one in the tail and two under the belly. Some plugs are one piece; others are jointed.

RATCHET. A mechanism that is built into the reel which, when set, makes a clicking noise when a fish takes the line, notifying the fisherman that he has a strike. It also slows down the speed of the line as the fish swims away with the baited hook.

REEL SEAT. A hollow tube metal extension of the small end of the rod butt on which the reel is secured by means of the reel clamps and screws. There is a hole in the end of the tube into which the rod tip is inserted.

REEL SPOOL. The cylindrical part of the reel upon which the fishline is wound.

RIG. A three way swivel arrangement. The fishline is attached to one swivel; the sinker to a second and the leader to the third.

ROD BELT. A leather belt that has a pocket appended in front into which the butt of the rod is inserted when reeling in.

ROD TIP. The section of the salt water fishing rod which is inserted into the hole in the metal extension of the rod butt. It is from about 4 feet 5 inches to 6 feet 10 inches in length and is made of bamboo; glass; beryllium and copper.

ROD BUTT. The heavy section of the salt water fishing rod

which is held in the hand and on which the reel is fastened and into whose metal end the rod tip is inserted. The butt is generally made of hickory, rosewood or ash.

SAND SPIKE. A hollow metal tube about 10 to 12 inches long and 2 inches in diameter. It is stuck upright in the sand and the rod butt is inserted in the upper end.

SINKER. A lead weight of from ½ to 12 ounces, or more, that is attached to the end of a fishing line, its weight carrying the bait down to the desired depth of water. Sinkers are generally round, oval, bank (long and tapering) and pyramidal in shape.

SNELLED HOOK. The upper third of the shank is tightly wrapped with silk, nylon or cotton thread. This thread ends in a loop above the upper end of the shank, where the eye would normally be. This loop takes the place of the eye; the leader is attached to it.

SPINNER. A flat, shiny piece of metal of various shapes which, impelled by the action of the water, revolves around a thin metal bar to one end of which the leader is attached. On the other end is the hook.

SPINNING. Fishing with light tackle and a specially constructed reel whose spool does not revolve. The line runs off the end of the spool, impelled by the force of the cast. Due to the reel construction, a backlash is practically impossible.

SPINNING REEL. A type of reel in which the spool does not revolve, as in a standard reel. The line is spilled off of the end of the spool by the impetus imparted by the casting motion. The line is wound back onto the spool by a revolving pick-up arm that automatically sets the instant the reeling in process begins.

SPOON. A flat, shiny artificial lure similar in shape to the bowl of the common table spoon.

SPREADER. A piece of wire-like metal that terminates in an eye at each end. A leader is attached to either eye. The wire extends horizontally and equi-distant from each side of a metal center. The metal center has two eyes, top and bottom. The line is attached to the top eye, the sinker to the bottom eye. The wire spreader serves to keep the leaders and bait apart when in the water. *See illustration page 182.*

STREAMER. A fish hook with feathers attached to it. These can be of different kinds. It is very similar to a bucktail or regular feather lure.

STRINGER. A stout, heavy line with a length of pointed metal at one end and a metal ring or crossbar at the other. The pointed end is passed through the gills of the fish and then through the ring, or around the bar, looping the line and securing the fish. The fish can then be lowered into the water for keeping or carried by the Stringer.

STRIKE. When a fish hits and takes the lure or bait.

SURF FISHING. Fishing in the surf, i.e. where the swell of the ocean breaks along the shore.

TEST LINE. Originally based on a linen thread test, each thread that is built into a fishing line will stand a strain of 3 *pounds on a direct* pull. Thus a line made of 10 threads will stand the strain of a pull of 30 pounds; a line of 70 threads, a strain of 210 pounds, etc. without breaking.

TILT. A piece of wood about 12 inches long by 3 inches wide by ½ inch thick. Centered down its length is a springy strip of steel. This steel strip can be looped back and "set" with a trip, similar to setting a mouse trap. The fishline is attached to a small, revolving wood spool that is located about 4 inches from the top of the Tilt. There is a small, red flag that is controlled by the action of the steel strip. When the Tilt is "set" and a fish takes the line, the trip is sprung and the flag flutters out, attracting the attention of the fisherman, notifying him that a fish is on the line that is paying out off of the wooden spool. Before setting the trip, the Tilt is placed upright, imbedded in the ice.

TROLLING. Fishing from a constantly moving boat with the fishing line played out over or near the stern of the boat.

WADERS. Long pants made of rubber or canvas and rubber, which are waterproof. They come up to under the armpits, being held in place by suspenders over the shoulders. Those with felt soles are best for slippery rock fishing.

WOOD CORK. A very buoyant piece of wood, generally round, with a projection at both top and bottom. Each projection has an eye near the end. The fishline is passed through both of these eyes thus keeping the Cork upright in the water. These Corks, or Floats, are usually painted two colors. Floating on the surface, they serve to keep the bait on the line below them suspended at any desired depth. They can be set at any point on the line.

WOOD FLOAT. This float is a top-shaped piece of wood about five inches long, one inch thick at end, one and a half inches at the other. It has a screw eye at each end. A leader is attached to one; the line to the other. This float can be used as added weight for casting if small plugs are the lure.

ELEVEN O'CLOCK POSITION. Picture yourself standing beside an upright clock, parallel to the right side. From a perpendicular position, drop the rod tip back to about 3 o'clock. Then snap the wrist forward and when the rod tip approximates 11 o'clock, stop the forward motion of the rod, as the line is released. Except on taking the tip back, the arm enters but very little into the motion.